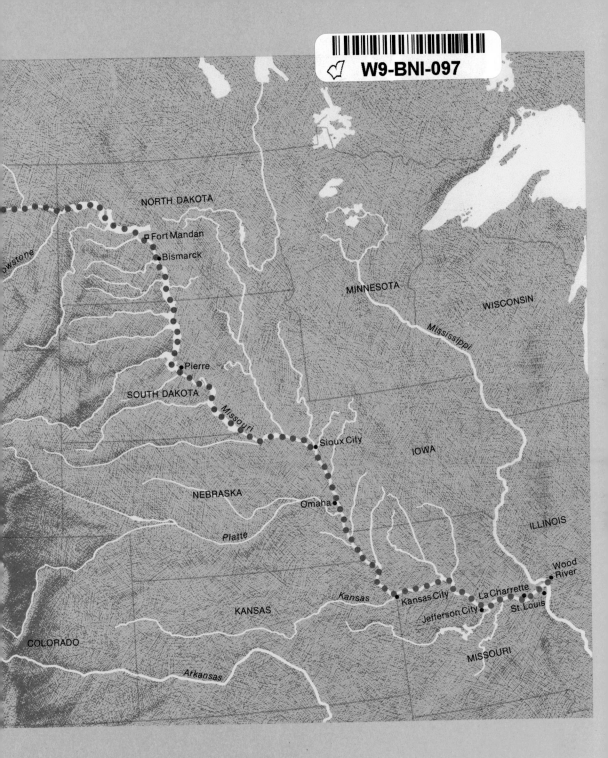

LEWIS AND CLARK EXPEDITION

the following spring, Lewis and Clark portaged the Great Falls of the
Missouri and crossed the perilous Bitterroot Range. At the Clearwater,
they resumed their river journey. Heading ever westward via the Snake
and the Columbia, they attained the Pacific Coast in November 1805.

In the Footsteps of Lewis and Clark

By Gerald S. Snyder

Photographs by Dick Durrance II

Illustrated by Richard Schlecht

Foreword by Donald Jackson,
Professor of History, University of Virginia
Produced by the Special Publications Division
Robert L. Breeden, Chief
National Geographic Society, Washington, D.C.
Melvin M. Payne, President
Melville Bell Grosvenor, Editor-in-Chief
Frederick G. Vosburgh, Editor

IN THE FOOTSTEPS OF LEWIS AND CLARK

By GERALD S. SNYDER,
National Geographic Staff
Photographs by DICK DURRANCE II,
National Geographic Photographer
Illustrated by RICHARD SCHLECHT

Published by
THE NATIONAL GEOGRAPHIC SOCIETY
MELVIN M. PAYNE, *President*
MELVILLE BELL GROSVENOR, *Editor-in-Chief*
FREDERICK G. VOSBURGH, *Editor*
GILBERT M. GROSVENOR, *Executive Editor*
  for this series
ANDREW H. BROWN, *Consulting Editor*
DONALD JACKSON, *Consultant*
  Professor of History, University of Virginia

Prepared by
THE SPECIAL PUBLICATIONS DIVISION
ROBERT L. BREEDEN, *Editor*
DONALD J. CRUMP, *Associate Editor*
LEON M. LARSON, *Manuscript Editor*
MARGERY G. DUNN, *Research and Style*

Illustrations
BRYAN HODGSON, *Picture Editor*
JOSEPH A. TANEY, *Art Director*
JOSEPHINE B. BOLT, *Assistant Art Director*
RONALD M. FISHER, LOUISE GRAVES,
  H. ROBERT MORRISON, GERALD S.
  SNYDER, *Picture Legends*
LINDA M. BRIDGE, *Picture Legend Research*
PEGGY WINSTON, *Research Assistant to the Artist*
GERALDINE LINDER, *Illustrations Research*
WILLIAM M. ALLAN, ISKANDAR BADAY,
  VIRGINIA L. BAZA, BETTY CLONINGER,
  BOBBY G. CROCKETT, JOHN D. GARST, JR.,
  Map Research and Production

Production and Printing
ROBERT W. MESSER, *Production Manager*
ANN H. CROUCH, *Production Assistant*
JAMES R. WHITNEY, JOHN R. METCALFE,
  Engraving and Printing
SUZANNE J. JACOBSON, DONNA REY
  NAAME, JOAN PERRY, SANDRA A. TURNER,
  Staff Assistants
ANN H. CROUCH, *Index*

*Surf whips the rugged Pacific Coast — goal of the
expedition led by Meriwether Lewis and William
Clark. Overleaf: Indians observe the Corps of Discovery in an 1896 painting by Charles M. Russell.
Page 1: Clasped hands and crossed tomahawk and
peace pipe on a Jefferson Peace Medal symbolize friendship between Indians and white men; scholars believe
the explorers presented this medal to a Mandan chief.
Bookbinding: Portraits of Lewis (left) and Clark
by Richard Schlecht after Charles Willson Peale.*

OVERLEAF: MACKAY COLLECTION, MONTANA HISTORICAL SOCIETY; PAGE 1:
COURTESY DR. KENNETH O. LEONARD (APPROXIMATELY 3/5 ACTUAL SIZE)

Foreword

When I was a boy, growing up near the banks of the Missouri, I thought of Lewis and Clark as western men. Then I moved to Illinois and discovered that the residents of Wood River, and of St. Louis across the Mississippi, felt rather possessive about these two explorers. Now that I live in Virginia, and Meriwether Lewis's birthplace is only a couple of hills away, I find that Virginians claim Lewis and Clark as their own.

Why, I have often wondered, does the story of the Lewis and Clark Expedition seem to belong to everyone? Why does each generation discover it again and tell it over and over?

Perhaps because it is everyman's daydream of ordinary men doing extraordinary, improbable things. The eastern city-dweller, who may never see the Bitterroot Range of the Rockies or experience a rainy winter along the Oregon coast, can read the narrative and suddenly become aware that superhuman feats do not always call for supermen.

For the Montana rancher, looking down upon a muddy reach of the Milk River in springtime, the experience is an even more personal one, because he lives in Lewis and Clark country—as do countless other Americans. To them, such landmarks as a clump of gnarled cottonwoods or a rocky prominence beside a stream are poignant reminders of our first great national venture into the unknown West.

We historians and other professional students have tried hard to make Lewis and Clark the objects of detached study. We have written of their medical practice, their work with newly discovered plants and animals, their compassionate observation of the Indians, and the impact of their expedition on our relations with Spain and Great Britain. But the story, the plain story of that exciting enterprise, inevitably wins out. It captures us all.

The narrative that Gerald S. Snyder has written, based on research and a personal retracing of the route with his family, is a fine combination of techniques. While he keeps us busy on the trail, he educates us as well to the scientific and geopolitical importance of the expedition. Perhaps, as a guest in the house, I can add what no National Geographic staff writer would say: Mr. Snyder has had the assistance of dedicated editors, researchers, and illustrations specialists who, like the rest of us, have fallen prey to the charm of a cast of characters—to the calm leadership of Meriwether Lewis, the unfailing competence and inspired spelling of William Clark, the courage and devotion of York and Sacagawea, and the hardiness and dogged accomplishment of such men as John Ordway, Nathaniel Pryor, George Drouillard, and the Field brothers.

No other story in our national experience is like this one.

DONALD JACKSON
Professor of History
University of Virginia

CHARLES WILLSON PEALE, 1807, 1810 (OPPOSITE), INDEPENDENCE NATIONAL HISTORICAL PARK, PHILADELPHIA

Contents

Westward Destiny

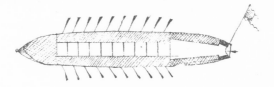

CHAPTER ONE

FOR MORE THAN A WEEK the young Army captain rode through the mire of crude trails that wound southeastward from his barracks in Pittsburgh. Finally, on the first day of April 1801, in high spirits, he reached the raw village of Washington. In his saddlebag Meriwether Lewis carried a letter from the President of the United States. "The appointment to the Presidency of the U. S.," Thomas Jefferson had written, "has rendered it necessary for me to have a private secretary."

In offering the post to his fellow Virginian, the President made it clear that he wanted no mere secretary. The job — at $500 a year — would be more in the nature of aide-de-camp: "Your knolege of the Western country, of the army and of all it's interests & relations has rendered it desireable for public as well as private purposes that you should be engaged in that office."

For the next two years Lewis would be treated as one of Jefferson's own family — sharing the company of poets, writers, scientists, diplomats, and politicians. At least twice each year the President would retreat to the rich red earth and rolling heights of Albemarle County that both he and Lewis loved. And there, 167 years after Jefferson assumed the Nation's highest office, I began my own excursion into history.

At Locust Hill, about seven miles west of Charlottesville, Virginia, and only ten miles from Monticello, I strolled with my wife Arlette and our

"...this being the day appointed by Capt. Clark....we fired our swivel on the bow hoisted Sail and Set out in high Spirits for the western Expedition. we entered the mouth of the Missourie haveing a fair wind Sailed abt. 6 miles...."

From the journal of Pvt. Joseph Whitehouse on departing Wood River, Illinois Country, May 14, 1804. Keelboat deck plan (above) from field notes of Capt. William Clark; Yale University Library.

two children, Michele, 6, and Daniel, 4, admiring the grace of wind-tossed leaves and the expanse of fields and woods that undulated toward the distant Blue Ridge Mountains. On this gentle knoll, in a rustic manor long ago burned to the ground, Meriwether Lewis was born in 1774. Even as a youth he would be remembered, in the words of a schoolmate, as a lad "always remarkable for perseverance . . . a great steadiness of purpose . . . and undaunted courage."

A proficient hunter, he often wandered alone across the wooded hills in quest of opossum and raccoon. Nearby, in Caroline County, another boy — four years older — was growing up with the same love of woods and fields and open spaces. Only in legend, apparently, did the two boys play together as children, but their lives were to join, their names to become inseparable. As partners in discovery, Lewis and the redheaded William Clark would journey farther into the largely unknown West than had any other American — forging up the Missouri River, struggling over the Rocky Mountains, and pressing on to the Pacific Ocean.

We would retrace the route of that expedition — Arlette, Michele, little Danny, and I — beginning the trail where they began it, where the Missouri pours into the Mississippi. Traveling by car and towboat, by canoe and rubber raft, on foot and on horseback, we would sample the steamy heat of a Missouri summer, the numbing cold of North Dakota at Christmas, and the chill and fog of the Pacific Coast in winter.

William Clark was too young for the Revolutionary War, but all of his brothers fought in it; his oldest brother, George Rogers Clark, won considerable fame in the Illinois Country in campaigns against the British forts at Kaskaskia and Vincennes.

It was to Gen. George Rogers Clark in 1783 — when William was only 13 — that the then Congressman Jefferson first put the idea of sending an explorer into the vast lands beyond the Mississippi. Although Jefferson was intrigued by the notion that prehistoric creatures might be roaming those empty spaces on the map, he also had the vision to realize that the river routes of the West might provide a feasible trade link with the Pacific. Ever since the 1500's men had been searching for a water route — a Northwest Passage — across the North American Continent.

The venture suggested to General Clark never materialized. But then came a fantastic scheme. In 1785, as U. S. Minister to France, Jefferson met John Ledyard, a Connecticut Yankee who planned to cross Russia and Siberia to the Pacific Ocean and seek passage on a Russian ship to the northwest coast of America. Beginning there, alone except for two dogs, the cocky adventurer planned to hike across the Rocky Mountains to the Missouri River and back to civilization.

Jefferson encouraged Ledyard, but the Russian Empress Catherine the Great called the plan "chimerical" and refused to let the American cross her land. Entering Russia of his own volition, Ledyard reached Siberia. In the city of Irkutsk the following winter, after traveling some 3,000 miles, he was arrested on Catherine's orders and ignominiously escorted across the Russian border into Poland.

But the idea of a river road to the Pacific continued to intrigue Jefferson, and in 1792 his hopes were recharged. He learned that Capt. Robert Gray of Boston had discovered the mouth of the Columbia River.

This time Jefferson, now President Washington's Secretary of State, worked through the oldest learned organization in the country, The American Philosophical Society Held at Philadelphia for Promoting Useful Knowledge—to use the full title—which Benjamin Franklin had founded in 1743. As the society's vice president, Jefferson helped raise funds to back a western journey proposed by the French botanist André Michaux. Meriwether Lewis, then 18, asked to go along, but Jefferson wanted the older, more experienced explorer to go alone. "Find the shortest & most convenient route of communication between the U.S. & the Pacific ocean," he instructed the Frenchman.

All Michaux found was a way to stir up trouble in the newly formed American Republic. Enlisted by the notorious Citizen Edmond Charles Genêt as a secret agent of the French Government, he got only as far as Kentucky before he was abruptly recalled.

Once again Jefferson's hopes had been dashed. Then came the disquieting news that on July 20, 1793, only five days after Michaux had left, Alexander Mackenzie and a small band of *voyageurs,* traveling under the British flag, had reached the Pacific by way of Canada's Peace and Parsnip Rivers. But theirs was no commercial route—the mountains were too high, the rivers too narrow. Jefferson could go on hoping.

And Meriwether Lewis went on looking for adventure. In 1794 he found it. That year, in the "whiskey counties" of western Pennsylvania, the Scottish and Irish settlers took up arms against the Federal Government, daring to take shots at officials who came to collect Alexander Hamilton's tax on the products of their stills.

When President Washington called out 12,000 militiamen to put down the rebellion, young Lewis, now 20 years old, volunteered for duty as a private. He saw no action—in the face of Federal troops the "Whiskey Boys" disbanded—but he found his calling.

Commissioned an ensign, the equivalent of today's second lieutenant, and assigned to the Second Sub-Legion of the Regular Army, Lewis was sent down the Ohio to join the troops of Gen. "Mad Anthony" Wayne.

"...explore the Missouri river, & such principal stream of it, as ... may offer the most direct & practicable water communication across this continent...."

Thomas Jefferson's instructions to Meriwether Lewis evolved from discussions between the President and his secretary. Here, they confer at Monticello.

Not long after, either in late 1795 or early 1796, he was reassigned to a rifle company commanded by Capt. William Clark. The two men became fast friends.

A family acquaintance later would remember Clark as a "youth of solid and promising parts, and as brave as Caesar." Joining the militia at 19, the young soldier rose quickly in rank. In 1790, just a year after he enlisted, he fought against the Creek and Cherokee Indians. Commissioned a lieutenant in the Regular Army the following year, Clark saw more action. Now a captain, he commanded one of the Army's elite infantry units.

In the beginning of their Army friendship, Lewis and Clark were not long together. On July 1, 1796, Clark resigned his commission—mainly to help untangle the confused business affairs of his brother George Rogers, who had pledged his own family's funds to support his campaigns in the Illinois Country.

While Clark the civilian toiled on the family farm in Kentucky, Lewis the soldier made frequent wilderness journeys. He took small units into Indian country, commanded a fort, and visited frontier posts as a regimental paymaster, traveling up and down the Ohio River. In 1799 he was promoted to lieutenant, and the following year to captain. In March 1801, after a routine swing through the Ohio Country, Lewis returned to his barracks in Pittsburgh to find the letter from Jefferson inviting him to come to Washington.

If the year 1801 was a good one for Meriwether Lewis, it was an ominous one for the United States. Napoleon Bonaparte had determined to restore the French colonial empire in North America, and in the spring of 1801 alarming news leaked from Europe: By the secret Treaty of San Ildefonso in October 1800, the Spanish Government had agreed to "retrocede" to France all of the province of Louisiana west of the Mississippi and give up the port of New Orleans as well. Instead of having the weak government of Spain on its western boundary, the United States now had a more lusty and aggressive neighbor, the greatest military power in the world.

"The day that France takes possession of N. Orleans," Jefferson wrote to the U.S. Minister to France, Robert R. Livingston, "fixes the sentence which is to restrain her forever within her low water mark," for by her action she "seals the union" between Great Britain and the United States. Jefferson urged Livingston to negotiate for the purchase of New Orleans and the colonies of East and West Florida. All of the commerce of the United States west of the Appalachian Mountains moved on streams that led into the Mississippi, and almost half of the Nation's produce passed through New Orleans to market.

In late November of 1802 came more grave news. The month before, the Spanish Intendant at New Orleans had withdrawn the United States' right of deposit—the permission to store goods awaiting shipment abroad. The closure order shocked the country, disturbed Jefferson, and infuriated many—some of whom demanded retaliation.

Napoleon was having his troubles too. Revolt rocked his West Indian island dependency of Santo Domingo, the base from which he would take forces to occupy Louisiana. France moved to put down the broad-scale insurrection begun by the Negro genius Gen. Toussaint L'Ouverture, but her troops fell victim to guerrilla warfare and yellow fever and finally met total disaster.

Jefferson sensed the emergency in French affairs. He called on his Virginia friend James Monroe, made him Minister Extraordinary and Plenipotentiary, and instructed him to prepare to sail to France to assist Livingston. On the success of his mission, Jefferson told Monroe, depended "the future destinies of this republic."

Then, more boldly, Jefferson moved again. On January 18, 1803, he sent a confidential message to Congress, asking for backing of an expedition into the West. To stem possible Federalist objections, he disguised his proposal as a "literary pursuit" — an effort to add to the geographic and scientific knowledge of the area. But to help persuade Congress to back the venture, he described its commercial advantages, skillfully alluding to the "great supplies of furs & peltry" that Indians on the Missouri River were furnishing England.

Frugally, Jefferson requested and received $2,500 — "for the purpose of extending the external commerce of the U. S." It was a paltry amount, far short of what the expedition would cost, but he had his wish.

Lewis would head the quest. Historians generally agree that Jefferson had discussed the expedition with his secretary a number of times during the previous year. Now, at last, they could carry it out.

*I*N FRANCE, Napoleon fumed. The debacle in Santo Domingo had cost him 50,000 lives. Realizing that his dream of a French North America would never be realized, the dictator declared, "I renounce Louisiana." But for the troublesome wilderness province there still could be a role, one he felt would help balance Britain's power in the war he now planned to wage against her. To deny Britain the opportunity to seize Louisiana, he would sell not just New Orleans, as Livingston had been asking, but the whole province, which he now felt was entirely lost. In the hands of the United States, at least, it would be "more useful to the policy and even to the commerce of France."

Though he knew Monroe was coming, the short-tempered Napoleon grew impatient. "Do not even await the arrival of Mr. Monroe," he ordered his Foreign Minister, Charles Maurice de Talleyrand-Périgord. "Have an interview this very day with Mr. Livingston."

For months Talleyrand had been stalling Livingston, toying with him, ignoring him. The American envoy anticipated that his meeting of April 11, 1803, would turn out to be another routine discussion. Then, to Livingston's utter astonishment, Talleyrand inquired, "What would you give for the whole?"

Monroe arrived in Paris the very next day, but neither he nor Livingston had the authority to buy more than New Orleans and the Floridas.

Napoleon left the negotiations to his Minister of Finance, Marquis François de Barbé-Marbois, who had lived in the United States and had the Americans' respect.

But what were Jefferson's emissaries to do about buying a territory virtually the size of the whole of the United States? Ships sailed slowly, so to communicate with Jefferson was out of the question.

Boldly, Monroe and Livingston accepted the challenge. They assumed responsibility for the Louisiana Purchase — "an event so portentous," Henry Adams would later write, "as to defy measurement."

Napoleon gloated: "This accession of territory strengthens forever the power of the United States and I have just given to England a maritime rival that sooner or later will humble her pride."

Into the domain of the United States, for 15 million dollars, now fell more than 830,000 square miles — the rivers, the mountains, the valleys, the forests, the ports, the prairies, the wildlife of a region of unmeasurable wealth, of unimaginable wonders.

At less than three cents an acre, it had to be one of the greatest real estate deals in history.

To make sure the treaty reached the United States safely, three couriers took copies, sailing aboard separate vessels. Jefferson had never dreamed of buying all of Louisiana, but when he heard the news, he called it "a transaction replete with blessings to unborn millions of men." On October 20, 1803, the Senate ratified the treaty.

The Louisiana Purchase, together with his many other achievements, ranks Jefferson among the greatest of all Americans. At the University of Virginia in Charlottesville I had a chance to get closer to the character of the man. Dr. Dumas Malone was at work on the fifth volume of his *Jefferson and His Time* when we met, and in his book-filled study at the university's Alderman Library we talked for an hour.

"Jefferson himself traveled no farther west than Staunton, Virginia, and never as far south even as North Carolina," Dr. Malone said. "But he explored in his mind. He had some illusions about the Noble Savage, some sentimentality, and in dealing with the Indians he tried to be humane, but he had to recognize that no power could stop the settlers. For the same reasons he believed that the United States was to get New Orleans, no matter who had title to it."

The historian paused occasionally to relight his pipe. I had the feeling as we talked that he so thoroughly knew the man that Thomas Jefferson might well have been sitting in the next room.

"The Louisiana Purchase was the most important single accomplishment of Jefferson's foreign policy," Dr. Malone continued. "Of course there was a large element of luck in it — the time was right — but it was the fruit of the consistent policy with respect to the Mississippi. His main concern was to get free navigation of the river, to get control of the waterways. He couldn't keep the Western States in the Union if he didn't have this."

Turning to the President's association with Lewis and Clark, Dr.

Malone explained: "Jefferson had a great regard and respect for young men all through his career. He treated them as his peers. And they had the greatest reverence for him. He trusted people."

It was with this trust that Meriwether Lewis now began the difficult task of preparing for the expedition. He needed men, boats, and supplies. Above all he needed a co-leader, someone he could trust, who would take over the full leadership should anything happen to him.

Lewis's choice was immediate: William Clark, his former commanding officer and friend. On June 19, 1803, with Jefferson's consent, Lewis wrote to Clark, telling him of the expedition and asking him to help find "some good hunters, stout, healthy, unmarried men, accustomed to the woods, and capable of bearing bodily fatigue in a pretty considerable degree."

Then came the great offer: "If therefore there is anything under those circumstances, in this enterprise, which would induce you to participate with me in its fatieues, it's dangers and it's honors, believe me there is no man on earth with whom I should feel equal pleasure in sharing them as with yourself."

Lewis waited for a reply for more than a month, but none came. The western mails were slow, he realized, but might Clark refuse his offer?

Lewis approached Lt. Moses Hooke of his own regiment, whom he described in a letter to Jefferson as "about 26 years of age, endowed with a good constitution ... industrious, prudent and persevering, and withall intrepid and enterprising." If Clark refused, Hooke would do.

Three days later, while Lewis was in Pittsburgh awaiting completion of a keelboat for use on the expedition, a reply from Clark arrived.

"This is an undertaking fraited with many difeculties," he wrote, "but My friend I do assure you that no man lives whith whome I would perfur to undertake Such a Trip."

Thus Moses Hooke missed his chance at immortality.

To Jefferson, only one man—Lewis—would be the supreme commander. Clark would be second-in-command. But Lewis couldn't bear to see his former commanding officer as his subordinate and offered Clark an equal role.

"My friend I join you with hand & Heart and anticipate advantages which will certainly derive from the accomplishment of so vast, Hazidous and fatiguing enterprize."

From a draft of a letter by William Clark confirming acceptance of Lewis's offer to join the expedition. In October 1803 they meet at Louisville, Kentucky.

When the War Department, in a flurry of red tape, ignored the request and made Clark a second lieutenant in the Corps of Artillerists, Lewis was furious: "it will be best to let none of our party or any other persons know any thing about the grade," he wrote Clark, "you will observe that the grade has no effect upon your compensation, which by G--d, shall be equal to my own." Throughout the entire journey Clark would remain a lieutenant, actually subordinate to Lewis in the eyes of the President, the Army, and the Secretary of War. But to the men of the mission, it would be Captain Lewis and Captain Clark.

More important, between the two officers there was no question that they would share equally in the command of the expedition.

By now Lewis had assembled much of the equipment he needed. From the U.S. Government arsenal at Harper's Ferry, in present-day West Virginia, he collected knives, tomahawks, rifles, flints, and gunpowder packed in waterproof lead canisters.

In Lancaster, Pennsylvania, he bought scientific equipment and took a cram course in celestial observation from an astronomer and surveyor, Andrew Ellicott. In Philadelphia, he spent $2,160.41; he bought more ammunition and firearms, as well as clothing, dried "portable soup," and bales of Indian presents — tomahawks, scalping knives, scissors, mirrors, beads, bells, brooches, calico shirts, rings, vials of vermilion, sheets of iron — and dozens of other items designed to please the Indians, whom Jefferson had ordered treated "in the most friendly & conciliatory manner."

There would be no doctor along, but in Philadelphia Lewis received medical advice from the naturalist and physician Benjamin Smith Barton, anatomist Caspar Wistar, and Benjamin Rush, then the most eminent physician in the United States.

WHILE IN PHILADELPHIA Lewis also received a letter from the President with detailed instructions for the upcoming expedition: "The object of your mission is to explore the Missouri river, & such principal stream of it, as, by it's course and communication with the waters of the Pacific ocean...may offer the most direct & practicable water communication across this continent for the purposes of commerce."

Preparing for our expedition, we too went to Philadelphia, and there visited the library of the American Philosophical Society. At a table outside the manuscript reading room Arlette took charge of the children, and I went with Murphy D. Smith, the assistant librarian, through the iron gate and thick steel door of the society's huge vault.

To follow the story of the expedition, I would use the classic eight-volume edition of the Lewis and Clark journals edited by Reuben Gold Thwaites. But now, back in the reading room, Mr. Smith spread out before me some of the society's greatest treasures — many of the original journals themselves, still in their bindings of red morocco and marble-patterned paper and cardboard.

With my notebook beside me, I turned the pages and followed the expedition day by day, noting the explorers' thoughts and feelings and sharing their adventures with them.

On August 31, 1803, Lewis and his little Corps of Volunteers for Northwestern Discovery pushed off from Pittsburgh down the Ohio River by keelboat, with 10 recruits, a river pilot, and a dog. At Louisville, Clark came aboard with his Negro slave York and several more recruits. Although it would be another nine months before the expedition actually began its journey up the Missouri River, one of the most exciting dramas in American history was under way.

Negro troops lynch French soldiers as rebellion sweeps the Caribbean colony of Santo Domingo. Napoleon's inability to stem the revolt cost him a strategic base for occupying Louisiana — retroceded to France by Spain in 1800 — thus helping to open the way for U.S. purchase of the western domain.

FROM MARCUS RAINSFORD, BLACK EMPIRE OF HAYTI, 1805

CRISIS AND TRIUMPH AT A COVETED PORT

Defiant Kentucky boatmen listen to an 1802 Spanish proclamation revoking their right of deposit in New Orleans. No longer could they use the port to store goods awaiting shipment aboard ocean-going vessels. Westerners, dependent upon New Orleans as their sole maritime outlet for the products of the Mississippi Valley, reacted angrily. Although Spanish authorities—who had not yet relinquished control of Louisiana—rescinded the order five months later, the furor it created already had focused attention on the importance of free navigation of the Mississippi River. Jefferson stepped up negotiations to buy New Orleans. Napoleon hesitated, but in 1803, forgoing plans for a French empire in the New World, he offered to sell all of Louisiana. An American eagle in a contemporary painting of New Orleans (opposite) symbolizes U. S. acquisition of the vast territory.

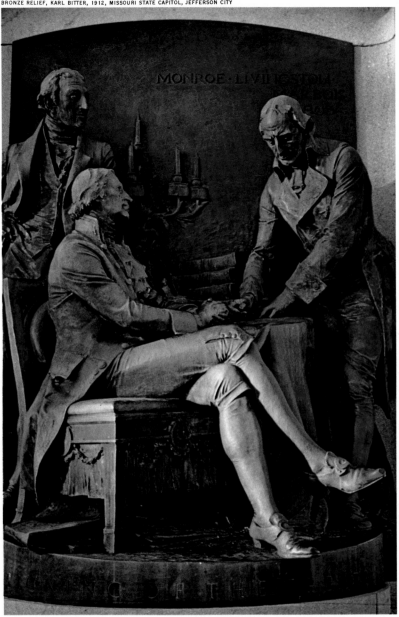

THE UNITED STATES BUYS AN EMPIRE

Napoleon's Minister of Finance, Marquis François de Barbé-Marbois, signs the Louisiana Purchase agreement in Paris. For U. S. envoys Robert R. Livingston (seated) and James Monroe, the action crowned one of the greatest diplomatic coups in American history. Dated April 30, 1803, but not signed until May 2, the treaty added some 830,000 square miles to the United States for $15,000,000, nearly doubling the Nation's size. The ill-defined boundaries of the purchase (oppo-site) extended roughly from the east bank of the Mississippi to the Rocky Mountains, and from northern Texas to just beyond the Canadian border. Believing that America's destiny lay in the West, Jefferson four months earlier had asked Congress for funds to send an exploration party to the Pacific. The Louisiana Purchase changed the nature of the expedition from a semi-secret intelligence mission to an open journey intent on commerce, settlement, and military defense.

(Original)

Treaty

Between the United States of America
and the French Republic

Done at Paris the tenth day of Floreal in the eleventh year of the French Republic; and the 30th of April 1803

R.R. Livingston

Barbé Marbois

Jas Monroe

Article 1

CANADA
U.S.A.
MONTANA
N. DAK.
MINN.
S. DAK.
Rocky Mountains
WYOMING
LOUISIANA
NEBRASKA
IOWA
PURCHASE
Mississippi
COLORADO
KANSAS
MO.
NEW MEXICO
OKLA.
ARK.
TEXAS
LA.
U.S.A.
MEXICO

BOBBY CROCKETT, GEOGRAPHIC ART DIVISION (ABOVE); NATIONAL ARCHIVES (TOP)

A PRICELESS PICTORIAL RECORD

Bison crowd along a valley as a herd descends from the arid grasslands of
the high prairie to drink from the Missouri; a few yards upstream a stag
stands guard over a gang of elk. The young Swiss artist Karl Bodmer portrayed the game-rich bounty of the Louisiana Purchase in 1833. Posing one
year earlier for Pennsylvanian George Catlin—first artist to travel into
the West—Blackfoot chief Stu-mick-o-sucks, or Buffalo Bull's Back Fat
(below), wore a tunic embroidered with porcupine quills and hung with
scalp locks. In 1898 cowboy-artist Charles M. Russell sketched his impression (right) of Lewis and Clark at Montana's Three Forks of the Missouri.

DIARIES OF HIGH ADVENTURE

During their 28-month journey, the explorers faithfully recorded details of what they saw. Clark's elk-skin-bound field book (above) contains rough notes he later transcribed onto permanent journal pages. Lewis, Clark, and at least five others kept diaries on the voyage. The expedition's artist and cartographer, Clark drew the cock of the plains, or sage grouse (right), discovered by Lewis on the Marias River in modern-day Montana, and sketched the Great Falls of the Columbia River (opposite), portaged in October 1805. He also showed how Chinook Indians along the Columbia gradually compressed the heads of their infants in a special cradleboard to give them a flattened appearance from the top of the head to the tip of the nose.

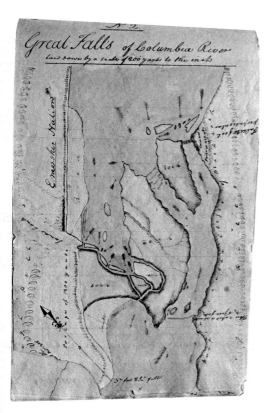

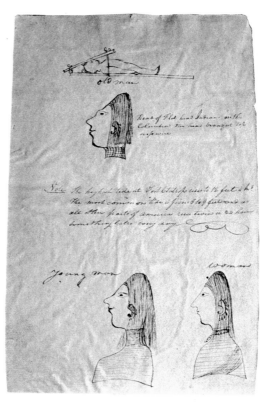

MEMENTOS THAT RECALL AN EPIC

Equipped with the best available arms, the expedition carried prototypes of the U. S. Rifle, Model 1803 (top). The weapon proved so effective that the Army later adopted the rifle as its first standard issue. An air gun, similar to one that the explorers carried, stored compressed air in a ball-shaped reservoir beneath the barrel; the novel piece could discharge 40 shots from a single load. Experts believe Lewis carried the English-made watch (below) during the journey; his iron for branding personal effects (opposite) turned up in 1894 along a bank of the Columbia River. Clark's wax seal bears his family coat of arms; the pocket compass (far right) also belonged to him.

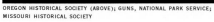

BLAZING A PATH THROUGH WILDERNESS

Deep into the uncharted West, Lewis (above) leads an advance party in search of the Shoshoni Indians. From the Shoshonis Lewis and Clark eventually obtained the horses that they needed to cross the fierce Bitterroot Range of the Rocky Mountains. Sacagawea, together with her husband Toussaint Charbonneau and their young son Jean Baptiste (opposite lower), traveled with the expedition from the Mandan Indian country of present-day North Dakota to the Pacific Coast and back. Although not the brilliant guide that she became in legend, Sacagawea served the voyagers well as a "token of peace" among the Indian nations. Clark's Negro slave York (opposite above) astonished many tribesmen who never had seen a black man; the captain eventually gave him his freedom.

A RIVER BECKONS A NATION WESTWARD

Sunrise gilds a reedy stretch of the Missouri near Omaha, Nebraska. Traveling up the broad river, Lewis and Clark opened the door to a newly acquired land. In their wake would come hunters, traders, soldiers, adventurers, and finally growing streams of settlers as the Nation moved inevitably toward the Pacific.

The Journey Begins

CHAPTER TWO

AT FOUR O'CLOCK IN THE AFTERNOON—with no more fanfare than the boom of a bow gun and a few huzzahs from "neighboring inhabitents" along the bank—the last of a fleet of three boats swung out from the mouth of Wood River, some 20 miles north of St. Louis in Illinois Country. Crossing the broad Mississippi, the vessels "proceeded on under a jentle brease up the Missourie." So, in William Clark's words, the "robust helthy hardy young men" of the Corps of Discovery began their epic journey on the 14th day of May 1804.

The twisting course of water has long since obliterated the original place of embarkation, but I sought out a marked site near that point. And there, across from where the Missouri now empties into the Mississippi, our own voyage started. As theirs was a military expedition, so ours appropriately commenced with the help of the Army. Aboard *Pathfinder*, a steel-hulled towboat of the U. S. Army Corps of Engineers, we sailed onto a Missouri River swollen by spring rains and melting snowpacks. Pieces of driftwood—and sometimes whole trees, their branches and roots reaching out weirdly—swept past.

Many Lewis and Clark buffs roamed the vessel, but to me one face especially stood out from the crowd—the image of a frontier hero. William Clark Adreon, whose freckled countenance called to mind portraits of his great-great-grandfather, walked the deck with me.

"...rived at St. Charls....an old french village Situated on the North Side of the Missourie and are dressy polite people and Roman Catholicks.... passed the evening verry agreeable dancing with the french ladies, &c."

From the journal of Private Whitehouse, May 16 and 18, 1804. Captain Clark sketched the rock painting (above), en route up the Missouri; American Philosophical Society, Philadelphia.

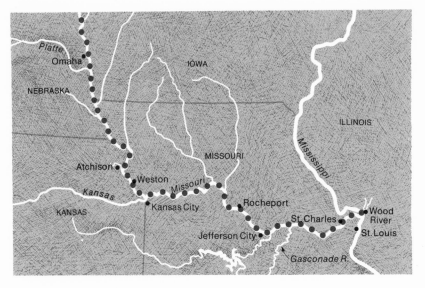

In two pirogues and a keelboat, the "robust helthy hardy young men" of the Lewis and Clark Expedition embarked from their winter camp at Wood River, opposite the mouth of the Missouri. Nine weeks later they reached the confluence with the Platte, 600 miles upstream in Indian country.

"The Corps of Discovery rode right up against debris just like this," he said, raising his voice over the rush of water and the thump of logs against the buoy barge linked to *Pathfinder*'s bow. "Imagine what it did to their boats. In those days the river's channel wasn't controlled by dikes the way it is now. It was more treacherous. And they had loaded the boats badly, heavy in the stern and light in the bow, so that they frequently ran up over concealed timber. At times it got so rough that they had to get out of the boats and drag them with ropes held from shore."

As our boat pressed onward, its diesel engines sending vibrations up through the deck, I climbed to the pilothouse. There I found my family chatting with the boat's master. Capt. Ruddle J. Spring had his left hand on the flanking rudder control, his right on the steering rudder, and his eyes on the buoys that marked the river's navigation channel. "We're going full throttle, but we can make only four miles an hour against this high water and fast current," he explained. "Normally, we could do about six and a half miles an hour upstream, but the river is extremely swift today, about as swift as it will ever get."

Against such a current the expedition also had labored; "the water excessively rapid, & Banks falling in," Clark wrote as the 55-foot-long keelboat *Discovery* and the two pirogues, or flat-bottomed dugouts, started up the Missouri. The keelboat of 22 oars carried a cannon at the bow, a cabin at the stern, and lockers with lids that could be raised to form a protective breastwork along the gunwales amidships. The pirogues—one of seven oars and painted red, the other of six oars and painted white— each mounted a blunderbuss which, like the keelboat cannon, could swivel in any direction.

A party of perhaps 47 composed the Corps of Discovery: 29 men of the permanent expedition, in addition to Lewis and Clark; on the red pirogue possibly 10 French *engagés*, hired to help carry stores and repel any Indian attack; and on the white pirogue an escort of six soldiers. They, like the Frenchmen, were to go only as far as the first winter encampment. Clark led the group toward St. Charles. There Lewis would catch up with the expedition, riding overland from St. Louis.

The men were ready for the hard life ahead. During five months of preparation in a log-cabin settlement at Wood River, they had been trained, outfitted, disciplined, and provisioned. Each man would add his own special talent to the odyssey—some as woodsmen, hunters, or carpenters; others as gunsmiths, cooks, boatwrights, or blacksmiths. A one-eyed Creole named Pierre Cruzatte and Pvt. George Gibson also would help to amuse the party and the Indians with their fiddling.

Next in command to Lewis and Clark was Sgt. John Ordway. He and the "nine young men from Kentucky"—Sgts. Charles Floyd and Nathaniel Pryor and Pvts. William Bratton, John Colter, George Shannon, John Shields, Gibson, and the brothers Reuben and Joseph Field—would form the backbone of the expedition.

Among the other men of the permanent party was a civilian, the expedition's scout, interpreter, and chief hunter, George Drouillard, whom Lewis had offered "25 $ pr. Month so long as he may chuise to continue with us." At 19, blue-eyed Private Shannon was the youngest and least experienced of the explorers; a spunky, barrel-chested Irishman from Pennsylvania, Pvt. Patrick Gass, at 32, was the oldest, with the exception of Clark.

Lewis and Clark would become, as one historian has put it, "the writingest explorers of their time." Both kept thoroughgoing journals. Although only a few fragments, on loose sheets, exist of Lewis's journal for the first vital months of the expedition, Clark's survives intact, together with many of his field notes; he kept a daily record for all but 10 days of the entire journey. Lewis also encouraged other members of the expedition to keep journals, and five—possibly six—did. Of these, four have survived—one only in a drastically edited version. The published journal of the untutored Gass bears obvious evidence of the heavy hand of the well-meaning Pittsburgh bookseller who would come to his aid.

*G*ASS VISUALIZED THE EXPEDITION passing "through a country possessed by numerous, powerful and warlike nations of savages, of gigantic stature, fierce, treacherous and cruel; and particularly hostile to white men." Campfire gossip, perhaps, for none of the other diarists thought to include a similar comment in his opening entries.

To Joseph Whitehouse, another of the privates who kept a journal, the men simply had "hoisted Sail and Set out in high Spirits for the western Expedition." "Sailed up the missouria," Floyd added. And Ordway, who kept his journal tucked beneath his shirt for safekeeping, remarked that "a number of Citizens see us Start."

Pvt. Robert Frazer also kept a journal, but it has never been found. If the other sergeant, the literate Pryor, wrote anything of the journey, it remains a mystery.

It has been said that Americans of Lewis and Clark's day not only had freedom of speech but "freedom of spelling." Once, when I showed some journal entries to my daughter Michele, she seemed puzzled by their curious style and remarked how "funny" many words looked. I explained that these men were more schooled in hunting and fishing and how to survive in the wilderness than in letters. "They spelled to reproduce the sounds of the words they were writing. And though they may have known little about commas and periods and the right way to spell, they were resourceful and clear-headed and intelligent men."

I delighted in the journals, not just for the facts of the mission that they contained, but for the small talk, for the descriptions of simple day-to-day occurrences, and for the charming, unpretentious way the diarists set them down. Arriving at St. Charles on May 16, Clark wrote: "a number Spectators french & Indians flocked to the bank to See the party. This Village is about one mile in length, Situated on the North Side of the Missourie....those people appear Pore, polite & harmonious."

It had taken *Pathfinder* seven hours to travel from the mouth of the Missouri to St. Charles—hardly more than a half-hour drive by highway. But it took Clark and his men two days to reach the same point.

The first permanent white settlement on the Missouri, St. Charles was already 35 years old when the keelboat and pirogues tied up at its riverfront on that Wednesday noon of 1804. Seventeen years later Missouri's first state legislature would convene here, but in 1826 St. Charles would give up the state capitol to Jefferson City, a rising upriver town.

When the expedition arrived, Clark warned the men that he expected them to "have a true respect for their own Dignity." But in the excitement of the nightlife that followed, some of the men forgot his words and suffered the consequences of their last fling. On the keelboat's quarterdeck, a court-martial convened the next day to try three errant enlisted men. Pvt. John Collins was charged with being absent without leave, "behaveing in an unbecomeing manner" at a dance held in the men's honor, and using disrespectful language on his return to the boat. The other two, Pvts. William Werner and Hugh Hall, each faced a single charge of having gone AWOL with Collins. The court recommended mercy for Werner and Hall, remitting their sentences of "twenty-five *lashes* on their naked back," but Collins got the full punishment—50 lashes at sunset.

Three days later, Lewis arrived during a thunderstorm, accompanied by many of his friends from St. Louis, and the drenched Newfoundland dog Scannon that he had bought in Pittsburgh.

On May 21, with the bulk of the expedition's stores and equipment shifted from stern to bow, the boats pushed off from St. Charles. "Set out at half passed three oClock under three Cheers from the gentlemen on the bank," Clark noted. Soon after, the group ran into a driving rainstorm that lasted "with Short intervales all night."

Encountering a group of friendly Kickapoo Indians the following day, Lewis and Clark gratefully accepted presents of four deer and gave the Indians two quarts of precious whiskey in return.

The second day out from St. Charles, Lewis left the keelboat to walk alone. Although both officers would take their turns away from the boats, Lewis — the introvert, aloof and melancholy, enjoying the freedom and solitude of the land — would do so more often. Clark — the extrovert, hearty and good-natured — preferred the company of the men.

Although they differed in temperament, rarely would two officers so perfectly share a command. Theirs was to become one of the most famous co-leaderships in American history. What one man lacked in talent the other possessed: Lewis, the more literate, the better educated, the better botanist and biologist, had the mind of a good scientist; Clark, the better cartographer and geographer, the better waterman and navigator, had a deep liking for Indians and a better understanding of them.

The partnership came dangerously close to an end before the voyage was 10 days old. On May 23 the expedition stopped to reconnoiter a cave, "Called by the french the *Tavern,*" at the base of a high cliff. Many others — Indians as well as white men — also had stopped there, as the names and "different immages" carved or painted on the sheer rock wall testified. Perhaps seeking a vantage point from which to survey the surrounding area, or possibly merely exercising his rambling instinct, Lewis decided to climb the steep cliff. At the very top he lost his footing. "Capt. Lewis near falling from the Pinecles of rocks 300 feet," the laconic Clark wrote in his journal, "he caught at 20 foot."

The idea of visiting the site had intrigued me since I first read about it in Clark's journal. For help, at St. Albans, Missouri, I turned to a local historian, one of that special breed of people who make a hobby of studying the heritage around them. With Mrs. Bernard J. Huger as our guide, we

"Honored Parence. . . . I am now on an expedition to the westward, with Capt. Lewis and Capt. Clark. . . . to ascend the Missouri River. . . . This has been our winter quarters. . . . will write next winter if I have a chance. Yours, &c. John Ordway Sergt."

From a letter written by Sergeant Ordway at Wood River, April 8, 1804

prepared to set out on foot. Soon a whole troop of history buffs had joined us, including Mrs. Huger's attorney husband, three of their daughters, a son-in-law, and a photographer and his son—nearly half as many as the permanent party of the Lewis and Clark Expedition.

We hiked eastward from St. Albans along the Rock Island Railroad tracks. Michele jogged ahead, and Danny as usual brought up the rear, occasionally hopping a ride for a shoulder-top view of the woods and hills around us and high cliffs to our right. We had gone about two miles when Mrs. Huger stopped and pointed to the top of the tallest bluff.

"About there," she said, "Meriwether Lewis slipped and fell."

The cave lay several hundred feet from the present course of the river. Once inside, Arlette and I paced off the floor and came up with the same dimensions as those reported by Clark—"about 120 feet wide and 40 feet Deep." We found no images painted by Indians, but we did find

"... the river riseing,
water verry swift ...
Current was so
Strong that we could
not Stem it with our
Sales under a Stiff
breese in addition to
our ores, we were com-
pelled to ... use the
Toe rope occasionally."
*From the journal of Captain
Clark, June 15, 1804, near
Malta Bend, Missouri*

on one wall three crudely carved letters, ORD, followed by much less distinct scratchings, possibly the date 1804. No one knows for sure, of course, but perhaps the journal-keeping Sergeant Ordway took time to leave his mark before the expedition once again pressed upstream.

A few miles above Tavern Cave, Lewis and Clark passed the small French village of La Charrette, which as Floyd pointed out was "the Last Setelment of whites on this River," the last outpost of civilization the expedition would see for almost two and a half years.

At La Charrette, Lewis and Clark met Regis Loisel, a trader and partner in the St. Louis Missouri Fur Company, who had been visiting Sioux villages far upriver. To the leaders of the expedition, Loisel appeared friendly enough—"he gave us a good Deel of information," Clark wrote. But just a few days later, Loisel was warning Spanish authorities about the danger of the expedition to Spain's trade among the Indians and to her claims to territory watered by the Missouri River and its tributaries. The Louisiana Purchase agreement contained no specific lines of demarcation, and some Spanish officials still viewed portions of the region as theirs.

Since Lewis and Clark first had organized their quarters at Wood River, the anxious Spaniards secretly had been eyeing the explorers' movements. As early as March, three months before the boats sailed, the Marqués de Casa Calvo, Spain's Governor General of Louisiana, had voiced fear of "the hasty and gigantic steps which our neighbors are taking towards the South Sea." The expedition must be stopped: "we must not lose time." He advocated the arrest of "the referred to Captain Merry and his followers" and the seizure of "papers and instruments that may be found on them." Just as the Corps of Discovery was to embark, the Commandant-General of the Interior Provinces, Brigadier Nemesio Salcedo, ordered a band of Comanches to spy on the expedition, "making efforts to apprehend it." But by the time the Indian party was fully organized, Lewis and Clark were beyond its reach.

*B*RACING FOR THE LONG VOYAGE, Lewis gave each of the sergeants duties on the keelboat — one at the helm to steer, arrange the baggage, attend to the compass, and "see that no cooking utensels or loos lumber of any kind is left on the deck;" the second in the center to "command the guard, manage the sails, see that the men at their oars do their duty," and, among other tasks, "attend to the issues of speritous liquors;" and the third in the bow "to keep a good look out for all danger which may approach, either of the enimy, or obstructions."

The sergeants rotated these duties and each oversaw a squad of eight, but Ordway kept the job of issuing staples ordered by the captains, "lyed corn and grece" one day, "Poark and flour" the next, and the day following "indian meal and poark." However, no pork was to be issued when fresh meat was available; their 50 kegs of meat, 14 barrels of parched corn meal, 20 kegs of flour, some 100 gallons of whiskey, together with smaller amounts of sugar, salt, coffee, dried apples, and biscuits, had to last as long as possible. Whenever they could, the men would live off the land, bringing in game on the backs of two horses led along the bank.

Reaching the Gasconade River on Sunday evening, May 27, Lewis and Clark set up camp on an island in the mouth of the stream. During the day they had encountered three groups of traders bound for St. Louis with furs obtained in trade with the Omaha, the Pawnee, and the Osage tribes, but learned nothing of consequence.

My family and I arrived at the mouth of the Gasconade in time to join the shakedown cruise of a Missouri River towboat. Its steel hull and wooden superstructure recalled the *Pathfinder,* but this vessel bore another proud name, *Sergeant Floyd.* When Michele asked why a whole boat was named for Floyd, I begged her patience; she soon would find out.

Just then the boat's master, Capt. Leonard W. Thompson, tooted the

Floyd's whistle. As he eased her out of the landing toward the Missouri, huge patches of sediment from the Big Muddy's banks turned the green Gasconade brown. "See how muddy the Missouri really is," Michele said when the contrast became apparent.

Returning from an eight-mile cruise downstream, we drove north on roads adjacent to the explorers' route—our eyes now on Meriwether Lewis and William Clark most of the way. Signs with silhouettes of the two explorers, which we would find along highways of 10 states, are one result of the work of the Lewis and Clark Trail Commission. For five years, from 1964 to 1969, this group formed by Congress promoted public awareness of the expedition and spurred a greater appreciation of the land along the route.

Up to the land of the Mandans, through known terrain, Lewis and Clark would carry the best available maps; but with none of the buoys, the flashing navigation lights, the embankment markers available to river voyagers today, they soon were in for trouble. On June 4, near the future site of Jefferson City, Ordway steered the keelboat too close to the bank. As the unhappy top sergeant told it, "the Rope or Stay to her mast got fast in a limb of a Secamore tree & it broke verry Easy."

So a small inlet got an apt if not a lasting name—Mast Creek.

The next stream they passed the captains called Nightingale Creek, after "a Bird of that discription which Sang for us all last night, and is the first of the Kind I ever heard," Clark reported. The bird's real identity remains a mystery. It couldn't have been a true nightingale; no species of this Old World bird has been known to exist in North America. Nor was it likely a cardinal—the so-called "Virginia nightingale"—because its song would have been familiar to Lewis and Clark.

With its mast mended, *Discovery* pressed on, now leading the pirogues into an area of sheer limestone bluffs too massive and strong to give way even to the unrelenting force of the river.

I had read much about the keelboat, of course, and studied paintings and drawings of her—even two sketches done by Clark himself. Now near the river town of Rocheport, Missouri, we had an opportunity to travel on a vessel similar in appearance to the *Discovery*. Arriving at a riverside recreational area called the Lewis and Clark Frontier, we spied the 15-star flag the United States had adopted in 1795 fluttering atop the mast of an excursion boat. Fifty-five feet long, she had a square-rigged sail, two swivel guns, a stern pole rudder, and long oars. But the steel cables in place of ropes and the navigation lights, fire extinguishers, and life preservers seemed incongruous.

"Lewis and Clark didn't have to worry about modern Coast Guard safety regulations," explained the boat's owner, R. J. Muntzel, who greeted us when we scrambled aboard. As Danny dashed for one of the swivels, a dull, laboring sound revealed the presence of other modern conveniences—beneath the rough cypress planking that hid the vessel's steel hull were two powerful diesel engines.

Upstream we chugged, past cliffs 150 feet high, and I turned to a volume

of the journals I carried with me throughout our trip. Not far from here on June 7, Clark wrote, the men stopped to explore a curious rock and "found it a Den of Rattle Snakes." They killed three, then investigated the rock to find it embellished with Indian pictographs "of the Devil and other things," thought Floyd, who added: "George Druer Kild one Bar" — the expedition's first bear, the black *Ursus americanus.*

On June 12, farther upstream, the explorers met a group of Frenchmen coming downriver on two rafts, one loaded with furs and the other with buffalo grease and tallow. The captains bought 300 pounds of grease for cooking, at five cents a pound, and then discovered that one of the raftsmen, Pierre Dorion, was a veteran frontiersman and Sioux interpreter who had known the Sioux for some 20 years and spoke their language fluently. Lewis and Clark persuaded Dorion to turn back with them — "as fur as the Soux nation with a view to get some of their Cheifs to visit the Presdt. of the United S."

The going grew rougher. Sunken snags, stiff breezes, driftwood, and shifting sandbars threatened to overturn the boats. When the current became too swift and the men could no longer row, they cordelled from shore. Already some of the party suffered from boils, others from dysentery. Clark observed that the Missouri's infernal muddy water contained "half a Comon Wine Glass of ooze or mud to every pint."

More than anything else, the men complained of insects. "The Ticks & Musquiters are verry troublesome," Clark observed on June 17, and again the next day, "The Musquiters verry bad." Attempting to repel the pesky bugs, the men smeared their bodies with cooking grease.

"... Current exceedingly strong ... boat against Some drift & Snags ... This was a disagreeable and Dangerous Situation, particularly as immens large trees were Drifting down ... the boat was off in a fiew minits...."

From the field notes of Captain Clark, June 9, 1804

But not even the hordes of mosquitoes could take away from the beauty and wonder of the country through which the men traveled. Surveying the surrounding area with Drouillard on June 21, Ordway reported he "never Saw as fine Timbered land in my life nor Such Rich handsome bottom land." That evening, Clark noted, the sun set remarkably, with "every appearance of wind, Blue & White Streeks centiring at the Sun as She disappeared and the Clouds Situated to the S.W. Guilded in the most butifull manner." The area teemed with wildlife. Above the mouth of the Kansas River nine days later, Clark wrote in his field notes, "Saw a verry large wolf on the Sand bar this morning walking near a gange of Turkeys....Deer to be seen in every direction and their tracks are as plenty as Hogs about a farm."

From Rocheport, we drove westward toward Kansas City, Missouri. As a complex of industries suddenly became a part of our trail, Arlette—a French citizen turned naturalized American—wondered if Lewis and Clark had ever imagined any of this. "You know, I'm not even sure I did seven years ago," she said, referring to the time when she first came to the United States. "But what impresses me most is not the big buildings and the industries, but the way the countryside seems so unchanging. There are so many hamlets and small towns—so much like Europe."

Pausing to check the journals, I found that Clark gave about as much space to their arrival at the future site of Kansas City as he did to "a large rattle Snake, Sunning himself in the bank."

For us the land now became more rolling, the rich loess flecked with the "brown gold of Missouri"—Burley tobacco that grew as seedlings under large polyethylene sheets spread to provide warmth and moisture. "I thought tobacco grew only in the South," Arlette said as we saw more and more of these tobacco beds.

About halfway between Kansas City and St. Joseph, we stopped at Weston, Missouri, a settlement first staked out in 1837. On Main Street, near high rock walls dating to the 1840's and '50's, I parked to seek out someone who could tell me about the history of the town. Try the Felling Clinic, someone suggested, and I did, happy to find that Dr. Ray J. Felling, the town's only doctor, was also the chairman of the Platte County Lewis and Clark Committee.

A tall, mustachioed man, whose collection of artifacts filled a glass-fronted cabinet in his waiting room, he paused between appointments to inform me, "Weston is a town of about 1,200 to 1,400 people, a quaint type of town, the only tobacco auction market west of the Mississippi. We have three tobacco warehouses where the planters' crops are sold at auction from the late part of November to January. Most of our buildings were constructed prior to the Civil War." And then, as though to underscore his town's role in history: "On July 2, 1804, the Corps of Discovery camped near what is now the foot of Main Street."

We crossed into Kansas, on the other side of the river. An Atchison banker, Harry Hixon, chairman of the state's Lewis and Clark Trail Committee, took us a few miles north for a look at Independence Creek, which the explorers named on the Fourth of July. The captains had ushered in the day with a shot from the keelboat's cannon, and named another stream they passed "4th of July 1804 Creek."

For Joseph Field, Independence Day was especially memorable—a snake bit him. And since Lewis didn't know if the snake was poisonous, he took no chances. Seeking to deaden the pain and draw out any venom, he applied a poultice of bark and gunpowder, spreading these substances on a small cloth and placing them on the wound.

In 80- and 90-degree temperatures the men pushed on, streams of sweat pouring from their backs. When Frazer suffered sunstroke, Clark watched as Lewis bled him and gave him niter, the relatively harmless potassium nitrate commonly known as saltpeter. The dosage "revived him much," Clark wrote.

*S*TILL MORE IRRITATIONS nettled the expedition. Five men became sick with "a violent head ake," and discipline once more had become a problem. On June 29 a keg of whiskey placed under the care of sentry John Collins proved too great a temptation for a fellow private, Hugh Hall, who induced Collins to relax his guard so he could steal some. Both men were caught and judged guilty by a court-martial. The explorers always looked forward to an occasional dram, so to them the theft of whiskey warranted severe punishment. The five-man court, consisting of Pryor, Colter, Gass, and Pvts. John Newman and John B. Thompson, ordered that Hall draw 50 lashes "on his bear Back" and Collins twice that number because he had been on duty.

Two weeks later, still another private, Alexander Willard, was charged with "Lying down and Sleeping on his post," a capital offense. Persistent in their determination to maintain discipline, the captains sentenced the court-martialed Willard to 100 lashes on his naked back—25 each evening at sunset for four consecutive days.

Early on the morning of July 14, after "some hard Showers of rain," the expedition set out, only to find the sky again growing dark. The wind blew fiercely, pushing the keelboat toward a sandbar. The men leaped out and with cable and anchor steadied the craft until—suddenly—the storm ceased, and "the river," Clark wrote, "become Instancetaniously as Smoth as Glass."

A week later the explorers arrived at the broad mouth of the great Platte River, which rises in the Rocky Mountains and flows into the Missouri below present-day Omaha.

In Indian country now, they stood on the doorstep of the upper Missouri, and 10 miles past the mouth the party camped. They planned, in Clark's words, "to delay at this place ... and Send for Some of the Chiefs ... to let them know of the Change of Government the wishes of our government to Cultivate friendship with them, the objects of our journy and to present them with Some Small presents."

The expedition's first council with the Indians was only days away.

Letter of credit from Jefferson to Lewis pledges "the faith of the United States" and financial backing for the expedition. Had it been possible for the explorers to return from the West Coast by ship, the letter would have paid their passage.

MISSOURI HISTORICAL SOCIETY

Dear Sir   Washington. US. of America. July 4. 1803.

In the journey which you are about to undertake for the discovery of the course
and source of the Missisipi, and of the most convenient water communication from
thence to the Pacific ocean, your party being small, it is to be expected that you
will encounter considerable dangers from the Indian inhabitants. should you
escape those dangers and reach the Pacific ocean, you may find it imprudent
to hazard a return the same way, and be forced to seek a passage round by sea,
in such vessels as you may find on the Western coast. but you will be without
money, without clothes, & other necessaries; as a sufficient supply cannot be carried
with you from hence. your resource in that case can only be in the credit
of the US. for which purpose I hereby authorise you to draw on the Secretaries
of State, of the Treasury, of War & of the Navy of the US.. according as you may find
your draughts will be most negociable, for the purpose of obtaining money or
necessaries for yourself & your men: and I solemnly pledge the faith of the
United States that these draughts shall be paid punctually at the date they
are made payable. I also ask of the Consuls, agents, merchants & citizens of any
nation with which we have intercourse or amity, to furnish you with those sup-
-plies which your necessities may call for, assuring them of honorable and prompt
retribution. and our own Consuls in foreign parts where you may happen to be, are
hereby instructed & required to be aiding & assisting to you in whatsoever may be
necessary for procuring your return back to the United States. And to give more
entire satisfaction & confidence to those who may be disposed to aid you, I Thomas
Jefferson, President of the United States of America, have written this letter of
general credit for you with my own hand, and signed it with my name.

                                                    Th: Jefferson

To   Capt. Meriwether Lewis.

O. E. BERINGHAUS, STATE OF MISSOURI (TOP); TARDIEU, THE BOATMEN'S NATIONAL BANK OF ST. LOUIS (ABOVE); ANNA MARIA VON PHUL, 1817, MISSOURI HISTORICAL SOCIETY

ECHOES OF FRANCE
IN LOUISIANA

Bucolic Ste. Genevieve drowses on a bank of the Mississippi some 55 miles south of St. Louis. Founded about 1735, Ste. Genevieve depended for its livelihood upon river traffic and nearby lead mines. Passing the settlement in 1803, Clark described it as a village of "about 120 familes, principally French." A French map of St. Louis, drawn in 1796, emphasized military fortifications. Carts like the one at right hauled produce on busy streets.

GRACIOUS LIVING ON THE EDGE OF CIVILIZATION

Well-to-do French lead miner, merchant, and planter, Louis Bolduc built a home in Ste. Genevieve around 1787 that survives today. Restored in 1956-57, the home illustrates the roughhewn but sturdy construction of early French houses in Louisiana. In the kitchen (above) a fire blazes in a stone fireplace hung with cooking utensils. Leaf-shaped racks used for parching corn hang from the ceiling. Authentic period furnishings re-create a frontier atmosphere. One end of the *galerie* — or porch — that rims the house on three sides encloses the kitchen (opposite above). Rush-seat, ladder-back chairs sit beneath windows and solid shutters typically French; no two of the locally made chairs have identical splats. Behind them, *poteaux-sur-sole* construction of the walls shows clearly: vertical oak timbers set on a stone sill with interstices packed with *bousillage* — a filling of clay and straw. Boys of Ste. Genevieve grew up to become boatmen in the trade with New Orleans. Canoes; pirogues, and flatboats hauled cargoes of lead and pelts to the cosmopolitan French city.

A WINTER CAMP, A FOREST PRIMEVAL

"...wintered at the enterance of a Small river opposit the Mouth of Missouri Called Wood River," Clark recorded in his journal. The explorers took care to establish their camp on the U. S. side of the Mississippi to avoid offending the Spanish in Louisiana. They remained here from December 1803 until mid-May of 1804. Above, November's leaves carpet a bank of the Mississippi near their point of departure. Opposite, members of a scientific expedition that 29 years later retraced part of the trail of Lewis and Clark gather around a campfire in a sketch by Karl Bodmer. The artist accompanied the party headed by German naturalist Prince Maximilian of Wied-Neuwied as it traveled through Missouri, the Dakotas, and into Montana. His paintings recorded with infinite care and remarkable accuracy the Indians, wildlife, and landscapes along the upper Missouri.

FROM RIVERS AND PLAINS,
ANIMALS NEW TO SCIENCE

Glossy-coated beavers gather twigs and branches for their riverbank lodge on the Missouri. The explorers encountered great numbers of this new species, the Missouri beaver, from the Platte River onward. They found beaver steaks a delicacy and set traps whenever possible. Their dams intrigued Lewis: "... willow brush mud and gravel ... so closely interwoven that they resist the water perfectly." The flat-tailed rodents would soon act as a powerful magnet to further exploration of the West. Beaver hats had grown in popularity since Beau Brummel appeared in London wearing one. Trappers and hunters quickly cut into the abundance that Lewis and Clark found; 29 years later Prince Maximilian rarely saw a beaver. The American badger (right) "never was Seen by any of the party before," according to Private Whitehouse. Clark wrote: "his head Mouth &c is like a Dog with its ears cut off ... it has a white Streake from its nose to its Sholders." It fed, he said, "on Bugs and flesh principally the little Dogs of the Prarie" like those at far right. Clark described the first encounter with prairie dogs: "the Village ... Contains great numbers of holes on the top of which those little animals Set erect make a Whistleing noise and whin allarmed Step into their hole."

AVERAGE HEAD AND BODY LENGTHS: MISSOURI BEAVER 36-40"; AMERICAN BADGER 24-33"; PRAIRIE DOG 13-16"

A RIVERSIDE SANCTUARY

Ghostly stone face yawns from Tavern Cave near the Missouri River hamlet of St. Albans, Missouri. The cavern sheltered Indians and white fur trappers long before Lewis and Clark passed by on May 23, 1804. One wall displays the letters ORD, believed carved by the expedition's Sgt. John Ordway. Since obscured: the "many different immages . . . Painted on the Rock at this place" that Clark saw.

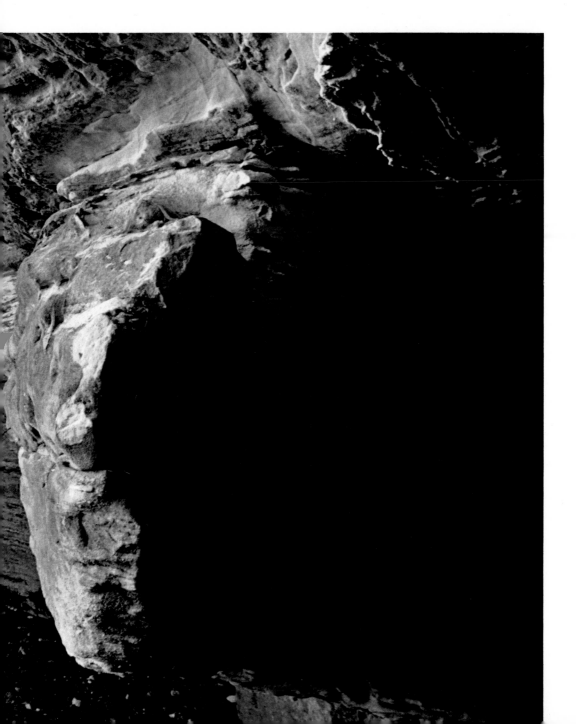

OBEYING A TIMELESS IMPULSE

Southward-bound geese erupt from the Squaw Creek National Wildlife Refuge, a 6,800-acre preserve in northwestern Missouri. A quarter of a million geese pause here annually. Near this point Lewis saw "great numbers of Goslings."

INTO PLAINS INDIAN COUNTRY

Indian braves congregate on a hill overlooking the mouth of the Platte River
(foreground) as it joins the Missouri. George Catlin, who set for himself the task
of "rescuing from oblivion the looks and customs of the vanishing races of native
men in America," painted the scene in 1832. At the Platte the explorers found
"the Sand bars much more numerous and the quick or moveing Sands much
worst." Similar sands clog the tangled waters of the Missouri near Vermillion, South Dakota (right). Camping 10 miles above the mouth of the Platte,
the party delayed to meet with Oto and Missouri Indians in a formal council.

Into Sioux Country

CHAPTER THREE

"PREPARED THE PIPE of Peace verry flashey," Clark wrote on August 1. Except for the few Kickapoos they had met on the lower Missouri, the explorers had seen no Indians during more than 600 miles of river travel. But now Lewis and Clark were no longer just explorers. They were ambassadors eagerly awaiting answers to urgent questions: Would the Plains tribes meet them in peace? Would they accept the white men's presents? Would they submit to the Great Father in Washington?

The answers were not long in coming. At sunset on August 2, a delegation of Missouri and Oto Indians rode up through the tall grass, accompanied by a Frenchman who had been living with them and had learned their language. The captains greeted the group and said they "were glad to see them, and would speak to them tomorrow." Clark added, "every man on his Guard & ready for any thing."

The following day, under an awning fashioned from the keelboat's mainsail, Lewis and Clark met with six chiefs of the two tribes. A "council"—the Louisiana Purchase negotiation—had been held with the French and Spanish, the captains explained. The red men's old fathers had "gone beyond the great lake towards the rising Sun," never to return. A new Great Father would be their Chief.

Each of the chiefs made a speech in reply. They were "no oreters," Clark recognized, but they liked the white men's talk and "wer happy to

"...as Soon as I landed...three...Men Seased the Cable...the Chiefs Soldr. Huged the mast, and the 2d Chief was verry insolent both in words & justures ...of Such a personal nature I felt My self Compeled to Draw my Sword...."

From the journal of Captain Clark, September 25, 1804, near Pierre, South Dakota.
Keelboat ensign (above) from Clark's field notes; Yale University Library.

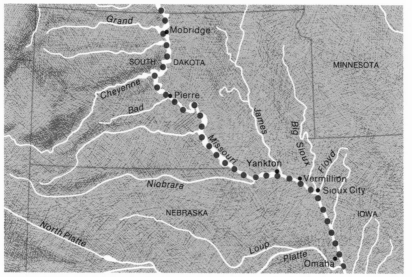

Near Omaha, Lewis and Clark met in their first council with a group of Plains Indians. Pushing northward, they smoked with the Yankton Sioux, and later, at the mouth of the Bad River, they encountered the notorious Teton Sioux. Ahead lay lands of the Arikaras and Mandans.

find that they had fathers which might be depended on." After passing the peace pipe, the captains hung medals around the necks of their guests and gave out paint, pieces of cloth, gunpowder, "& a Drop of milk" —a bottle of the white man's whiskey for which most Plains Indian tribes had developed a taste. The captains named the site of the confrontation "Councile Bluff," but when Clark wrote the words on his map he placed them—probably for convenience—on land that would one day become a part of the State of Iowa. Although an important Iowa city today bears the name Council Bluffs, the actual "Councile" site is on Nebraska soil, about 15 miles north of Omaha.

With my family I traveled there to walk about some of the countryside where Lewis and Clark had walked. Near this quiet line of bluffs, where mounds of earth heaped up by pocket gophers today dapple the rising ground, Lewis and Clark had met with the six chiefs. And from a high point such as this Clark had observed "the most butifull prospect of the River up & Down." I looked for some sign of the same scene he had described, but I could barely see the river; over the years the great Missouri has looped and twisted away from the bluffs until now it flows some two miles to the east.

Calling the children from their wanderings, Arlette and I prepared to retrace our path and visit the Joslyn Art Museum on the western edge of Omaha's business district, almost directly on the route of the Lewis and Clark Trail. Once inside we quickened our pace, passing up paintings by Monet, Renoir, and Pissarro so we could spend more time with the renowned artist-explorers of the 1830's: George Catlin, Karl Bodmer, and Alfred Jacob Miller. Seeing the work of these men—their sketches, oils, and watercolors—sharing something of their feeling for the unspoiled wonders of the frontier, both Arlette and I felt saddened that Lewis and Clark had taken no artist with them.

Northward we turned once more, into open country. We would see other excellent collections of western art along our route, but not until we neared the Pacific Coast would we encounter a city even half the size of Omaha.

In the town of Decatur, Nebraska—population 800—we stopped at a gas station and asked directions to "Blackbird Hill." Lewis and Clark and a party of 10 had ascended the hill, apparently out of the same curiosity that made us want to see the place where the great "King" of the Omahas had been buried.

The attendant seemed surprised. "It doesn't amount to anything any more," he said. "Nothing there, just a wheat patch and an old wooden cross sticking out of the ground."

We still wanted to see the place. Beyond Decatur we turned off the highway onto a dusty, winding road, stopping once to let a pheasant amble across our path, and again to chat with a friendly farmer. He offered to lead us the rest of the way in his truck.

Reaching the hill, we found neither cross nor wheat patch; only waving wild grass covered the promontory. Here in 1800, Omaha Chief Blackbird had been buried astride his favorite horse under a great mound of earth 12 feet around and 6 feet high. By his dying command, according to legend, Blackbird had ordered it. Thus in death as in life he would be able to keep watch for the boats of white traders. In his heyday the notorious chief had exacted heavy tribute from those early voyagers on the Missouri by confiscating some of their goods.

As the Lewis and Clark Expedition moved slowly upriver, the French engagé La Liberté decided to live up to his name. Sent to look for Indians before the men reached the Council Bluff site, he never returned. Being a hired hand, he was not pursued in force, but when Pvt. Moses B. Reed failed to return after pleading he had to go back to a camp already abandoned "to Git his Knife," as Sergeant Floyd put it, something had to be done. Lewis and Clark dispatched four men—George Drouillard, Reuben Field, William Bratton, and Francis Labiche—to bring back their fellow soldier dead or alive.

*S*OON APPREHENDED, Reed returned to face a court-martial. He was found guilty of desertion and sentenced "to run the Gantlet four times through the Party & that each man with 9 Swichies Should punish him and for him not to be considered in future as one of the Party," but as a common laborer.

The day ended on a happier note, with "an extra gill of whiskey and a Dance untill 11 oClock," for it was the 18th of August 1804, Meriwether Lewis's 30th birthday.

The merriment proved short-lived. The following day, as the boats fought their way upstream once again, Clark penned in his journal: "Serjeant Floyd is taken verry bad all at once with a Biliose Chorlick we attempt to relieve him without success as yet, he gets worst and we are much allarmed at his Situation, all [give] attention to him."

For some three weeks the sergeant had been suffering the effects of what was thought to be a bad cold. But this was no mere cold. The next day, August 20, he grew still weaker. Clark could detect no pulse. "Nothing will Stay a moment on his Stomach or bowels," he wrote, and quickly the captains ordered the boats to land. Gently the men placed Floyd in a heavy woolen blanket and carried him to the bank.

"I am going away," Floyd whispered to Clark. "I want you to write me a letter." A little while later the sergeant died. The men took his body to the highest bluff they could find, and there, over a crude grave lined with rough oak slabs, Lewis read the funeral service on ground that would become part of the State of Iowa.

"We buried him," wrote Clark, "on the top of the bluff 1/2 Mile below a Small river to which we Gave his name." The river remains the Floyd today; and nearby, a small town, Sergeant Bluff, also honors the soldier in memory.

"Did Sergeant Floyd have to die?" Michele asked. "Wouldn't a doctor have been able to save him?"

Months before, I had discussed this question with a physician friend who also is a student of Lewis and Clark. He told me that the captains had done about all that any medically trained man of the day would have been able to do. Lewis shared his mother's interest in herb remedies, and the well-versed Clark knew how to set broken bones, remove bullets, and treat a wide range of diseases. But surgical practices of the period were limited almost entirely to the extremities and surface of the body, with the blood-letting lancet serving as the best friend of many doctors.

"Most physicians who have studied Sergeant Floyd's symptoms today believe his death probably was due to a ruptured appendix," my friend had explained. "Since the first such successful operation did not take place until more than 40 years later, it's unlikely that even the best doctor in the country could have saved him."

We crossed the Missouri from Nebraska into Iowa. Near Sioux City we came upon Sergeant Floyd's grave, its monument towering above a bluff that overlooks the river. There to meet us was the chairman of the Iowa Lewis and Clark Trail Committee, Edward Ruisch, accompanied by Erman N. Swett of South Sioux City, Nebraska, a retired school superintendent who also had researched the story of the expedition. They told me how Floyd's remains had been moved twice and then finally placed under the sandstone shaft in 1901.

"In 1857 the rampaging river cut into the bluff and opened the grave," Mr. Ruisch told me. "A boy was lowered over the side by a rope to remove the remains. They were placed in a coffin and reburied in an unmarked grave farther back on the bluff."

Rediscovered in 1895, they were reinterred, placed in urns under a marble slab until the dedication of the monument six years later. "You know," he added, "this is the first designated national historic landmark in the United States."

We drove through Sioux City and across the Big Sioux River toward Elk Point, one of South Dakota's oldest communities. Near here in 1804

Clark reported finding a "great deel of Elk Sign" as the expedition halted to pick a successor to Sergeant Floyd. Of the three privates nominated — Bratton, Gass, and Gibson — the men elected Gass, the barrel-chested Irishman from Pennsylvania.

Stopping next in the town of Vermillion, we paused for rolls and directions at Jacobsen's Bakery on East Main Street. "Spirit Mound? Sure, I can tell you how to get there," the lady behind the counter said in a voice that seemed to question why we would want to take the trouble. "We live here the year around, but we never think about going to see it."

Such was not the case in the day of Lewis and Clark. According to Indian legend, evil spirits — little men about 18 inches tall with remarkably large heads — inhabited the mound. Armed with sharp arrows, they supposedly killed anyone who drew too near. "So Much do the ... neighbouring nations believe this fable," Clark reported, "that no Consideration is Suffecient to induce them to approach the hill."

Driving north from Vermillion we rounded a curve to see the mound rise suddenly as a single grassy eminence above the flat prairie.

The explorers had climbed the hill on an oppressively hot August day after a long overland hike. Clark noted that Scannon became "so Heeted and fatigued we was obliged [to] Send him back to the Creek."

Many of the men, Lewis among them, complained of thirst and stopped frequently to rest. Even the strong York had trouble keeping up, "he being fat and un accustomed to walk as fast as I," as Clark put it in his field notes.

A fresh breeze swept the hill the day we climbed it, and no one dropped out. We saw no little men. "Did Lewis and Clark?" Danny wanted to

"...proceeded to the trial of Reed, he confessed that he 'Deserted & stold a public Rifle Shotpouch Powder & Ball'...only Sentenced him to run the Gantlet four times through the Party & that each man with 9 Swichies Should punish him and for him not to be... one of the Party."

From the journal of Captain Clark, August 18, 1804, south of Sioux City, Iowa

know; I assured him they didn't. From the summit we looked out over some of the same "butifull landscape" that had enthralled Clark. Here the explorers had observed huge herds of buffaloes. In their place we found black Angus and white-faced Hereford cattle feeding in a rancher's pen.

Returning to their boats, Lewis and Clark pushed on, stopping to set fire to the prairies "as a signal for the Soues to Come to the River." Knowing that Indians were near, the captains grew worried over the possible fate of the young and inexperienced George Shannon, who failed to return from a hunting trip. He finally rejoined the explorers after a 16-day absence, having gone "12 days without any thing to eate but Grapes & one Rabit, which he Killed by shooting a piece of hard Stick in place of a ball," Clark reported.

The hapless Shannon had mistaken an Indian trail for that of the voyagers and had forged far ahead of the boats, leading the usually terse Clark to philosophize: "thus a man had like to have Starved to death in a land of Plenty for the want of Bullitts or Something to kill his meat."

To find and help summon the Sioux, the captains sent Sergeant Pryor and Pierre Dorion with presents of tobacco, corn, and kettles. And finally during the last two days of August, under a spreading oak near a flagstaff from which fluttered the Stars and Stripes of the young Nation, the captains met in a Grand Council with about 70 representatives of the Yankton Sioux.

"The Souex is a Stout bold looking people, (the young men handsom) & well made," Clark wrote, "the greater part of them make use of Bows & arrows, Some fiew fusees [muskets—Ed.] I observe among them, notwith standing they live by the Bow and arrow... the Warriers are Verry much deckerated with Paint Porcupine quils & feathers, large leagins and mockersons, all with buffalow roabs of Different Colours. the Squars wore Peticoats & a White Buffalow roabe with the black hare turned back over their necks and Sholders."

The captains extolled the Great Father, distributed medals, clothes, and a U.S. flag, and presented the Grand Chief with a richly laced American Army uniform complete with cocked hat. Then, said Clark, "We Smoked out of the pipe of peace."

Lewis couldn't resist the temptation to show off the expedition's novel air gun, and when he fired a few shots at a tree, the Sioux ran to examine the ball holes. They "Shouted aloud at the Site of the execution She would doe &c," penned Whitehouse.

As night fell, a circle formed around three fires, and the Indians began to dance. As Whitehouse told it: "they Gave a houp before they commenced dancing, they would dance around the fire for Some time and then houp, & then rest a fiew minutes. one of the warrirs would git up in the centre with his arms & point towards the different nations, & make a Speech, telling what he had done, how many he had killed & how many horses he had Stole &c. all this make them Great men & fine warrirs."

Next morning the chiefs arranged themselves for another powwow, this time "with elligent pipes of peace all pointing to our Seets," Clark wrote. The pipes, or calumets, so impressed the captains that they named the site "Calumet Bluff."

After the ceremonies the explorers departed, but without Pierre Dorion, who had agreed to stay behind for a special mission—to help "bring about a peace between the Suoex and their neighbours."

Today Calumet Bluff anchors the powerhouse of the Gavins Point Dam, one of a series of huge, lockless barriers that have transformed the Missouri River for a thousand miles into a chain of "Great Lakes."

At Yankton, Kenneth Jones, chairman of the South Dakota Lewis and Clark Trail Committee, and I boarded a small workboat of the Corps of Engineers for an outing on Lewis and Clark Lake, created by the dam.

As we traveled the two miles across to the Nebraska shore, our vessel churned up the first white water I had seen on the muddy Missouri. Boats of fishermen dotted the lake.

I learned that the water abounds with catfish, sauger, crappie, paddle-fish, white bass, and carp—many of the same species of fish that Lewis and Clark's men had caught with bush drags woven of willows.

The same day, some 50 miles farther upstream, I stopped at the St. Paul's Indian Mission at Marty, South Dakota, where about 400 Indian children—mostly Yankton Sioux—board while attending grade school and high school. Learning of my interest in Lewis and Clark, Father Francis Suttmiller, O.S.B., volunteered to guide me to some of his favorite haunts along the Missouri.

"From Yankton to here," he said, as we stopped for a closer look at the

"...a Seeder post with the Name Sergt C. Floyd died here 20th of august 1804 was fixed at the head of his grave. This Man at all times gave us proofs of his firmness and Determined resolution to doe Service to his Countrey and honor to himself...."

From the journal of Captain Clark, August 20, 1804, near Sioux City, Iowa

river, "there is one of the biggest concentrations of bald eagles in the United States. They congregate in the bluffs from December to January. In one day I counted 36."

The area called to mind one of Lewis's infrequent entries in the early journals. Walking along the river on September 17, the captain "found the country in every direction for about three miles intersected with deep revenes and steep irregular hills of 100 to 200 feet high." The description still fits much of the river-bluff country of South Dakota.

Lewis also observed other things — a country "still farther hightened by immence herds of Buffaloe, deer Elk and Antelopes which we saw in every direction feeding on the hills and plains." He did not think he exaggerated when he estimated "the number of Buffaloe which could be compre[hend]ed at one view to amount to 3000."

Midway through South Dakota, I too had an opportunity to see the great American bison. Near the state capital, Pierre — pronounced "Peer," to Arlette's astonishment — I stopped at the 50,000-acre Triple "U" Standing Butte Ranch. Jerry Houck, dressed in dungarees, chambray shirt, muddy boots, and cowboy hat, greeted me, and after a chat we climbed into the cab of his pickup truck.

For a mile or so we traveled over rolling, hilly grassland without seeing a single buffalo. Then suddenly hundreds of them appeared in all directions. Houck explained that he runs a herd of 1,500 buffaloes, bred commercially for meat.

He also raises cattle, but he finds buffaloes easier to manage. "They take care of themselves," Jerry told me. "Buffaloes will live where a cow will die. They will eat snow in place of water and will root down through the snow to get at grass and weeds, while a cow will starve to death with food only inches from its nose. Buffaloes won't overeat, they can survive in severe cold, and they have fewer disease problems."

When I left Standing Butte, thoughts of buffaloes still shuffled through my mind — thoughts of an estimated 60 million that had roamed the land during the days of Lewis and Clark. The Indians killed them by the thousand with their lances and bows and arrows, or by stampeding them over cliffs. But it was the white man with his rifle who killed them by the million for their hides, their carcasses, their tongues, and often just for pleasure.

The period of greatest slaughter occurred in the 1870's and early 1880's. By the end of 1882 the great northern herd had been reduced to a remnant. Finally, 26 years later, the United States established its first national bison range to protect the endangered beasts.

Back in Pierre, I turned again to the Lewis and Clark journals. Not far downstream, I learned, the expedition narrowly had escaped disaster. On September 21 the sergeant on guard suddenly noticed that chunks of the river-built sandbar on which the men lay sleeping had begun to slide into the water. Frantically, he gave the alarm.

Scant minutes before the entire sandbar sank into the river, cut to pieces by the rushing current, the men scrambled off and pushed away

Richard Schlecht

" . . . by the light of
the moon observed
that the Sand had
given away both
above and below our
Camp & was falling
in fast. I ordered all
hands on as quick as
possible . . . by the
time we made the
opsd. Shore our
Camp fell in. . . ."
Journal of Captain Clark,
September 21, 1804, near Fort
Thompson, South Dakota

in their boats. For the rest of the night they slept on the firm ground of
the opposite riverbank, grateful to be alive.

Four days later the expedition came face to face with the Teton Sioux,
well known for their harassment of trading parties. At the mouth of the
Bad River, about seven miles below today's Oahe Dam, Lewis delivered
his now-standard speech to a group of tribal chiefs.

Except for the sandbar incident, things recently had been going well
for the explorers, so well that the day before they had named an island
they passed Good Humored Island. But now, with the Tetons, trouble
stirred. It began as the captains invited the chiefs out to the keelboat and
gave them some whiskey. When one of them feigned drunkenness—to
cloak his "rascally intentions," explained Clark—the captain quickly took
the guests back to land in one of the pirogues.

As the vessel touched the bank, three young Indians seized the boat's cable. Another hugged the mast, and a chief called The Partisan, "verry insolent both in words & justures," staggered up against Clark. The chief had not received enough presents; the expedition could not continue!

For the first time hostile Indians threatened the Corps of Discovery. Clark drew his sword.

On the keelboat Lewis ordered the men under arms. The swivels pointed shoreward. The 50 or 60 warriors began stringing their bows and drawing their arrows. For the explorers to back down now, to show any sign of weakness, might be disastrous.

Though surrounded, Clark stood his ground, ordering the pirogue back to the keelboat for reinforcements. A dozen armed men quickly jumped aboard and rowed ashore to help the captain.

Never before had the Teton Sioux faced such resistance from a group of white men. They began to back off, and seeing this, Clark offered his hand to the few who remained. When they refused, he calmly turned to board the pirogue. He had not gone 10 paces when four Indians—two chiefs and two warriors—waded out after him, making signs that they wished to come aboard. The danger now over, Clark permitted them to accompany the expedition a short distance upstream. But the explorers still felt uneasy, and another island they passed received a name that reflected their mood of the moment: Bad Humored.

Not until the next day, when scores of braves, women, and children crowded the bank, did the Indians' reason for wanting to accompany the captains become apparent. Being good family men, they simply had wanted to show off the boats to their tribal households.

Lewis took five men and went ashore with the Sioux, whom Clark thought "disposed to make up & be friendly." But when, after three hours, Clark didn't hear from his co-leader, he became worried "for fear of Deception & Sent a Serjeant to See him." The sergeant came back with news that the captain was well, and Lewis soon followed. Then Clark took his own turn ashore. "On landing," he remembered later, "I was receved on a elegent painted B.[uffalo] Robe & taken to the Village by 6 Men & was not permited to touch the ground untill I was put down in the grand Concill house on a White dressed Robe," an honor usually reserved for very great chiefs.

Returning for Lewis, the Indians brought him back the same way, seating both captains at the side of the principal Sioux chief. Another peace-pipe ceremony was about to begin. The chief rose and "with Great Solemnity took up the pipe of Peace," wrote Clark, "& after pointing it to the heavins the 4 quarters of the Globe & the earth, he made Some disertation." His speech concluded, the chief lit the pipe and "presented the Stem to us to Smoke."

For an hour they smoked, until dark, and then they all gathered around a fire while 10 Indian musicians beat on skins stretched over hoops. The women began to dance, waving poles decorated with the scalps of Omahas their warriors had slaughtered two weeks before. The ferocious

Sioux had destroyed 40 Omaha lodges, massacred 75 men, and taken 48 prisoners—"Womin & boys which they promis both Capt. Lewis and my self Shall be Delivered up to Mr. Durion," Clark wrote.

As the little fleet prepared to set out again, a helmsman let his pirogue get too close to the keelboat, breaking its anchor cable and sending the vessel into the swift current. Loudly, Clark ordered "all hands up & at their ores," and in the excitement one of the Indians yelled that the "Mahars," or Omahas, were attacking. Within 10 minutes 200 Sioux warriors lined the bank. Forewarned that trouble might occur—the day before one of the Omaha prisoners had whispered that the Sioux intended to stop the expedition—the captains decided to camp, waiting for daylight to drag for the submerged anchor. A strong guard stood by in the boats throughout the sleepless night.

The next morning, failing to find the anchor, the men prepared again to cast off. Suddenly a group of warriors seized the keelboat's cable and demanded tobacco.

Lewis refused; he would not be forced into anything, and even "was near cutting the cable with his Sword and giving orders for the party to fire on them," witnessed Whitehouse. But eventually the captain relented, and threw a portion to the chief.

Giving the tobacco to his warriors, the chief "jurked the rope from them and handed it to the bowsman," wrote Clark; "we then Set out under a Breeze from the S.E."

"...on landing I was receved on a elegent painted B.[uffalo] Robe & taken to the Village by 6 Men & was not permited to touch the ground untill I was put down in the grand Concill house on a White dressed Robe."
From the journal of Captain Clark, September 26, 1804, near Pierre, South Dakota

The explorers had had enough of the Teton Sioux. Four miles upstream they stopped for the night, fixing "2 large Stone to our boats to answer as ankers," Ordway recounted, "as we did not intend to Camp on Shore again untill we Got to an other Nation."

As September turned into October, the men pressed northward. Reaching the Arikaras, Lewis and Clark went into council with the chiefs, making their usual speeches, giving out flags, medals, uniform coats, cocked hats, paint, and tobacco. But it was Clark's servant York who most interested the tribesmen. Never having seen a black man before, they gathered around and "examind him from top to toe," Clark noted.

A bit of an actor, York told the Arikaras that he had been a wild animal until caught, and appalled them with tales of having eaten young children. Clark later confessed that his servant had "made himself more turribal than we wished him to doe."

The Arikaras of Lewis and Clark's day were an agricultural people who lived in earth-lodge villages. They tended their gardens, made pottery, and hunted buffaloes with bow and arrow—and occasionally warred with their neighbors.

*C*URIOUS about visiting Arikara village sites that lay along the Missouri, I stopped at Mobridge, South Dakota, and called on Dennis Loose and Marion Travis, the president and vice president, respectively, of the Northern Oahe Historical Society. They told me that the remains of perhaps as many as 75 villages had been inundated by the massive reservoir that backs up for 250 miles above Oahe Dam.

"I'd just as soon see the old river bottom where you could go and pick chokecherries and blueberries like Lewis and Clark did," Mr. Travis lamented as we drove toward one of the few sites still above water. It was obvious that scores of the pothunter variety of amateur archeologist had been there before me, but a few bits and pieces of artifacts still remained —a bone flesher here, some pieces of incised pottery there, a pitted hammerstone, even a hoe made from a buffalo shoulder blade. How much more, I wondered, rested at the bottom of the reservoir.

As the expedition left the Arikara nation on October 12, they took with them a chief, Arketarnashar, who wanted to "make a good peace" with the Mandans to the north.

The next day Pvt. John Newman—possibly in a moment of depression —uttered some mutinous expressions. Lewis arrested him on the spot, and that night a court-martial was summoned and "9 of his Peers" found him guilty and "Senteenced him 75 Lashes and banishment from the party." When the men stopped on a sandbar and carried out the flogging, Arketarnashar was horrified. His nation "never whiped even their Children, from their burth."

The disgraced Newman became just a "labouring hand" on the red pirogue, but during the long winter ahead he would seek to atone for his thoughtless action.

Glowering under his headdress of magpie, raven and eagle feathers, Pehriska-Ruhpa leads a dance of the Dog Band, a society of Hidatsa warriors. Artist Karl Bodmer painted the portrait during his stay at Fort Clark in the winter of 1833-34. Lewis and Clark had wintered at nearby Fort Mandan 29 years earlier.

BRINGING THE BUFFALO NEAR

Mandan Indians brandish spears, clubs, and rifles in the buffalo dance — "all this is to cause the buffalow to Come near So that they may Kill them," wrote Clark in January 1805 of a similar dance at a village near Fort Mandan. Caught up in the frenzy of the exhausting celebration, a spectator fires his gun into the air.

KARL BODMER, 1833 (TOP) AND 1834, COLLECTION OF MR. AND MRS. PAUL MELLON

HOMES OF THE HUNTERS

Women ferry firewood across the Missouri River (above) in bullboats of buffalo skins stretched over wooden frames. Plains Indian women also gathered food plants, fetched water, and dressed hides; men hunted and waged war. In the background stand the earthen lodges of Mih-tutta-hang-kush, a Mandan winter settlement of about 60 families near the site of Fort Mandan. With the return of the buffalo in spring, the tribe moved into tepees. The light, portable dwellings housed the Sioux (left) year-round as they followed the herds. Between hunts, Sioux braves recount their deeds of valor; atop a funeral scaffold lies the cloth-wrapped body of a distinguished warrior.

PROUD WARRIORS ALONG THE MISSOURI

Decorated with honors of war, Mandan second chief Mato-Tope, or Four Bears, grips his iron tomahawk (opposite). The yellow stripes on his right arm represent deeds of valor in battle; the yellow hand shows he has taken prisoners in combat. A turkey feather and sticks in his hair signify wounds from an arrow and bullets; the wooden knife painted red recalls the slaying of a Cheyenne chief. "A warrior so adorned," wrote Prince Maximilian, "takes more time for his toilette than the most elegant Parisian belle." Bodmer captured strong personalities and bold features in his portraits of men of other Plains tribes that Lewis and Clark had encountered: a Missouri Indian (below left); an Oto (below right); an Assiniboin (bottom left); and a Yankton Sioux.

KARL BODMER, 1833: NORTHERN NATURAL GAS COMPANY COLLECTION, JOSLYN ART MUSEUM, OMAHA (OPPOSITE) AND COLLECTION OF MR. AND MRS. PAUL MELLON

SEEKING SPIRITS ON THE PRAIRIE

Ominous clouds (opposite) gather over Spirit Mound near Vermillion, South Dakota, recalling words from Clark's journal: "A cloudy morning Capt. Lewis & Myself concluded to go and See the Mound which was Viewed with Such turror by all the different Nations in this quarter." Indians believed the 100-foot-high mound harbored tiny spirit people — excellent marksmen who killed anyone who ventured too near. Although the explorers found no "unusial Sperits," from the top of the hill, they "beheld a most butifull landscape," wrote Clark. "Numerous herds of buffalow were Seen feeding in various directions; the Plain to North N.W. & N.E. extends without interruption as far as Can be seen." Today some unfenced, open country remains. Near Mullen, Nebraska, the Middle Loup River (below) meanders through the arid high prairie — a sea of rolling grasslands.

THE FIERCE TETON SIOUX

War party of the Teton Sioux celebrates a victory with a scalp dance (opposite). "No description that can be written could ever convey more than a feeble outline of the frightful effects of these scenes," said artist George Catlin. Above, a Sioux brave pulls against thongs tied to wooden skewers piercing his chest while he gazes at the sun. Such self-torture earned him the status of medicine man. Skillful hunters as well as warriors, the Teton Sioux killed grizzlies (below) for meat and grease — and for pleasure.

'SPIRIT OF FIRE' SWEEPS THE PLAINS

Fleeing a racing prairie fire, Plains Indians gallop along a buffalo trail through
tangled growth 8 feet high. Tribesmen often set such fires to encourage new grass.

A TRIUMPH OF GOOD OVER EVIL

Spectacle of blood and pain climaxes the annual Okipa ceremonies of the Mandans. Offerings to the Great Spirit, high on poles, loom over the "big canoe," a barrel-like structure in the center of the village representing a legendary ark that once saved mankind from a worldwide flood. A ring of yelling braves circles the canoe as a medicine man cries against it. Outside the ring, vol-unteers undergoing self-torture run the "last race," dragging buffalo skulls and weapons tied to skewers piercing their arms and legs; eventually the weights tear the skewers out through the flesh. During the two preceding days, while the initiates remained inside one of the lodges without food, water, or sleep, buffalo dancers (top right) performed around the ark. Other men

mimicked such creatures as the rattlesnake and the beaver (center right). On the fourth day, the evil spirit (bottom right) threatened the villagers until overcome by the power of the sacred medicine pipe. In addition to celebrating the end of the traditional deluge, the ceremonies petitioned the return of the buffalo herds and enabled chiefs to assess each warrior's strength and endurance.

GEORGE CATLIN, 1832: SMITHSONIAN INSTITUTION (LEFT)
AND COLLECTION OF MR. AND MRS. PAUL MELLON

Richard Schlecht

The First Winter

CHAPTER FOUR

SUMMER HAD PASSED. Chill winds from the north played over the land, bringing cold and numbing rain; at night crisp carpets of frost whitened the ground. Since its departure from Wood River more than five months earlier, the expedition had traveled some 1,300 miles, but now the first season of voyaging was nearly over. "The wind So hard a head the [boat] could not move," Clark wrote on October 17, "...the leaves are falling fast." And a week later: "Some little snow."

Lewis and Clark had planned to winter hundreds of miles farther up-stream, but frequent rest periods and long councils with the Indians had consumed 37 precious days. They would have to revise their plans.

On October 26, now deep into land that would become the State of North Dakota, the expedition camped below the first of two villages of Mandan Indians. There was little of the tension that had prevailed during the explorers' confrontation with the Teton Sioux three months before. Many Mandan "men womin & children flocked down to See us," Clark reported. With a group of principal chiefs as his guides, Lewis walked to the nearest village while Clark remained in camp.

Today the shifting channel of the Missouri has so altered the topography of the area that historians cannot point to the location of the sites of the two villages with any degree of accuracy. Near the modern-day town of Washburn, North Dakota, I stood on a snow-covered hill beyond

"...I with 15 men...killed 8 buffalow & one Deer, one Cow and calf was brought in...Several men returned a little frost bit...I felt a little fatigued haveing run after the Buffalow all day in Snow many Places 18 inches Deep...."

From the journal of Captain Clark, December 8, 1804, Fort Mandan, North Dakota. Captain Lewis drew the iron battle-ax (above) used by nearby Indians; American Philosophical Society, Philadelphia.

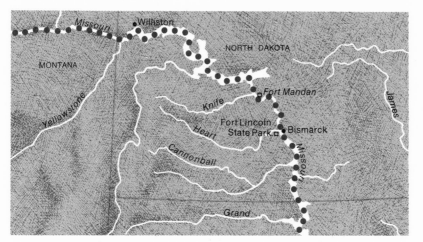

Where the Knife River joins the Missouri, the explorers felled cottonwoods to build Fort Mandan. Through the winter the men made clothing and moccasins, built boats, and questioned Indians and traders about the land ahead. On April 7, 1805, the expedition re-embarked, reaching the confluence of the Yellowstone and the Missouri Rivers 19 days later.

a curving ridge of the riverbank and looked out across the frozen fields and plains. Here, somewhere within my view — perhaps where tall trees now grow, or where the river flows — the explorers had sat in council with the Indians who would be their neighbors during the long, frigid winter that lay ahead.

Addressing the assembled tribal chiefs on "a fair fine morning after Brackfast," Lewis and Clark informed the Mandans and their neighbors the Hidatsas that they now had a new Great Father — a President who cared, who wanted to know about his Indian children, and who wished to help them. One of the Hidatsa chiefs grew restless as the captains delivered their speeches. Claiming that his village faced attack by hostile Indians, the haughty leader — nicknamed Le Borgne, or One Eye, by French traders — announced he had to leave; only when another chief rebuked him did he decide to stay.

He probably was glad he did because after the high-sounding oratory the officers bestowed numerous gifts on the chiefs: flags, medals, uniform coats, cocked hats, and even the expedition's heavy iron corn mill, which had promised to become only a burden to the explorers.

As it turned out, the Indians had ideas of their own about the use of the device. Visiting the Mandans in 1806, the Canadian trader Alexander Henry would find the remains of the mill "which the foolish fellows had demolished to barb their arrows; the largest piece of it, which they could not break or work up into any weapon was fixed to a wooden handle, and used to pound marrow bones to make grease."

That evening, following the council, the prairie caught fire. Two Indians died in the flames, three others were badly burned, and several more narrowly escaped injury, among them a half-breed boy thrown to the ground and covered with a green buffalo hide by his mother.

"Those ignerent people," Clark wrote, "say this boy was Saved by the Great Medison Speret because he was white." Whatever the reason, historians believe the incident may have supplied the idea for an episode in James Fenimore Cooper's novel *The Prairie.* In the story a Pawnee brave wraps himself in a buffalo hide to save his life in a prairie fire.

On November 2, after surveying the surrounding area, Lewis and Clark decided on the site for a fort where the expedition would spend the winter. It lay on the east bank of the Missouri about six miles below the mouth of the Knife River, near an area forested with tall cottonwoods and haunted by game. As the men swung their axes, curious Indians came to watch from a Mandan village four miles upstream.

Another who came was a French-Canadian trapper and fur trader, Toussaint Charbonneau. In his mid-forties, Charbonneau had spent most of his life in the Northwest, and for the past five years he had been living among the Hidatsas. When he asked to be taken on as an interpreter, Lewis and Clark quickly hired him.

A week later his Indian wife walked into camp — and into history. Young Sacagawea—"Bird Woman" in Hidatsa—had grown to girlhood among her people, the Shoshonis, in the Rocky Mountain foothills of present-day Montana. When she was about 12, a marauding band of Indians, possibly Hidatsas, invaded her village and carried her off. Traded from one warrior to another, eventually she was bought — or won in a gambling game as one story goes — by Charbonneau. Soon to bear Charbonneau's child, she would become the lone female member of the expedition.

APIDLY the fort began to take shape. Two rows of log-walled huts, joined four to a row, branched out at an angle, and a high, semicircular fence enclosed the wedgelike area not bounded by cabins. Two other huts within the compound were constructed to house provisions and stores.

About the middle of November, increasingly cold weather forced the men from their thin canvas tents into the encampment they called Fort Mandan. The westernmost military outpost in the United States had been built "so strong as to be almost cannonball proof," a Canadian trader observed.

Lewis and Clark shared a single cabin, and the rest of the men the other seven. Split-plank floors, raised about 7 feet off the cold ground, were covered with grass and clay to provide warm lofts for sleeping; the roofs were sloped shed-fashion to ward off snow; and cracks in the cabin walls were daubed with clay.

Returning from hunting forays, the men hurried indoors to warm themselves before the stone fireplaces of their cabins. New snow fell, and the weather grew still colder. Clark recorded the ordeal:

December 8: "the Thermometer Stood at 12d. below 0."

December 14: "the Murckerey Stood at 0 this morning."

December 17: "the Thmt. Stood a[t] 45° below 0."

If I had any reason before to question the accuracy of the expedition's thermometers, I didn't now. In my own journal — my notebook — I wrote:

December 21: "The temperature dipped to 4 below."

December 23: "Between seven and eight o'clock this evening the thermometer registered 12 below."

We wore layer upon layer of warm winter clothing, and at times we still felt the cold; how the men of the expedition endured in buckskins and handmade moccasins remains a mystery to me. Pvt. Thomas Procter Howard returned to camp one day with "his feet frosted," and some of the other men also suffered from frostbite, but not one man lost even a toe to the cold.

Checking the journals for "Christmas Tuesday," 1804, I read how the expedition celebrated. The Indians had been told not to visit the fort because this was one of the white men's "great medicine days." Proudly, the men hoisted the American flag and saluted it with a shot from the keelboat cannon. They passed the day in hunting, dancing, drinking, and feasting. Such a day must be observed "in a proper and social manner," as Sergeant Gass noted, and for dinner all manner of delicacies were distributed, including "flour, dried apples, pepper and other articles." It was the "Best to eat that could be had," wrote Sergeant Ordway. Three rounds of brandy were served during the day, and so it went, as Clark remembered, "until 9 oClock P.M. when the frolick ended &c."

We began our Christmas Day frolic by retracing our earlier route, driving southward to Bismarck, the capital of North Dakota, and across the Missouri to Fort Lincoln State Park. At Slant Indian Village, on the site of an abandoned Mandan settlement, five circular earth lodges have been carefully reconstructed to show how people of the tribe once lived. Here we would spend Christmas.

Inside one of the lodges we found a cottonwood-log fire already crackling. Our friends, Terry Eiler and his wife Lyntha, were preparing a blazing reception for a 14-pound buffalo rib which Harold Schafer, owner of the Blackburn Ranch upriver, had presented to us as a Christmas gift.

The lodge was the strangest house the children had ever seen, but a fine playground. Off they went, running around and between the structure's four great central supporting posts as Arlette and I sought to learn how the Mandans built their homes. We inspected the roof beams resting in forks of supporting posts, examined the willows laid over the rafters, and poked at the thick matting of dry grass that had been plastered on the framework of branches with loose, wet earth.

Despite the fire, it grew cold inside, and I thought of turning the lodge's buffalo-skin bullboat upside down, Indian fashion, and placing it over the open smoke hole. The Mandans, I knew, often used their bullboats to regulate drafts as well as to keep stray puppies from falling into the fire.

"Did the Indians knock before entering the lodge?" Arlette wondered aloud. In a sense they did, I learned later. Rattles of buffalo hoofs hanging from the door warned the occupants of anyone entering. The door itself, made of buffalo skin stretched over a willow or cottonwood frame, was placed inside the covered entrance passageway.

"Where did they sleep?" Michele asked.

"On beds of leafless willow branches covered with dry grass," I replied. "They wrapped themselves in buffalo-skin robes and used an old tepee covering padded with soft antelope hair for a pillow."

"Did they have horses?" Danny wanted to know.

I explained that horse racing was one of the Mandans' favorite sports. "They also liked to lasso wild horses from horseback while riding at full speed. They kept horses inside their lodges to hide them from enemies."

In 1750 as many as 9,000 of these peaceful Mandan Indians populated the region. They were an agricultural people who settled in villages, cultivating their plots of corn, beans, pumpkins, squash, and tobacco. In 1764 the first of a number of smallpox epidemics struck the tribe. Weakened by disease, the Mandans proved easy prey for the powerful Teton Sioux, who forced them to abandon their settlements and move farther north, where Lewis and Clark found them.

By 1804 the two villages the Mandans had established on the west bank of the Missouri had united, and the seven they had built on the east bank had been consolidated into five, then two, and finally a single settlement. Disease and enemy pillages had reduced the tribe to some 1,250. Merging with the Hidatsas, the Mandans eventually lost their identity as a separate tribe. Today not a single full-blooded Mandan lives.

We soon were joined by three guests who had come to share a part of our Lewis and Clark Christmas: James E. Sperry, archeologist for the State Historical Society of North Dakota, his wife Gail, and David O'Brien, director of the state park service, who had consented to our turning the lodge into a modern-day version of a Mandan feast site. Together the nine of us sat down to dinner on buffalo- and elk-skin robes.

"Some of the Natives went ... a hunting, in the evening as they were returning one of them gave out.... after they left him he came too ... his life was spared, but his feet was froze verry bad.... Capt. Lewis doctored him...."

From the journal of Private Whitehouse, January 9, 1805, Fort Mandan, North Dakota

The meat proved a little charred on the outside and a bit raw on the inside, but with its trimmings of baked potatoes, fresh apples and pears, and a fruit cake baked by Arlette and carried 1,330 miles from home, the dinner turned out to be a success, nevertheless.

With the meal each adult downed a dram of brandy, just as Lewis and Clark and their men had done.

For the expedition the arrival of the new year of 1805 occasioned still another frolic. The captains gave each man two rounds of "good old whiskey," Gass wrote. Then, "with their Musick"—a fiddle, a tambourine, and a tin trumpet—the men marched to the nearest Mandan village and square danced in various lodges until late in the afternoon.

But life at Fort Mandan was hardly all fun: "excessively Cold the

Murkery this morning Stood at 40° below 0," Clark wrote on January 10. Time and time again he reported, "Verry Cold. . . . a verry Cold Day. . . . A Cold Day Snow fell 4 inches deep." Through it all, the men passed the time in a hard struggle for food, in building canoes and making clothing and moccasins, in questioning the Indians about their language and customs, and in trading with them.

Most important, the explorers inquired of as many people as they could about the land ahead. Clark drew a map of the country — "from the information of Traders, Indians & my own observation & ideas." And from Indians who scratched their own crude maps on the ground with sticks, the captains learned of the Great Falls of the Missouri, much farther upstream, and of high mountains that barred the way to the Pacific.

Often during the long winter Clark noticed that the blacksmiths had "not an hour of Idle time to Spear," for the Indians would relinquish their precious corn only in exchange for aid in mending their weapons or for help in getting their "War hatchets Made." Busiest of all were the cap-

"The day fine, we Commenced very early to day the Cutting loose the boat which was more dificuelt than the Perogus with great exertions and with the assistance of Great prises we lousened her, and turned the Second perogue upon the ice. . . ."

From the journal of Captain Clark, February 24, 1805, Fort Mandan, North Dakota

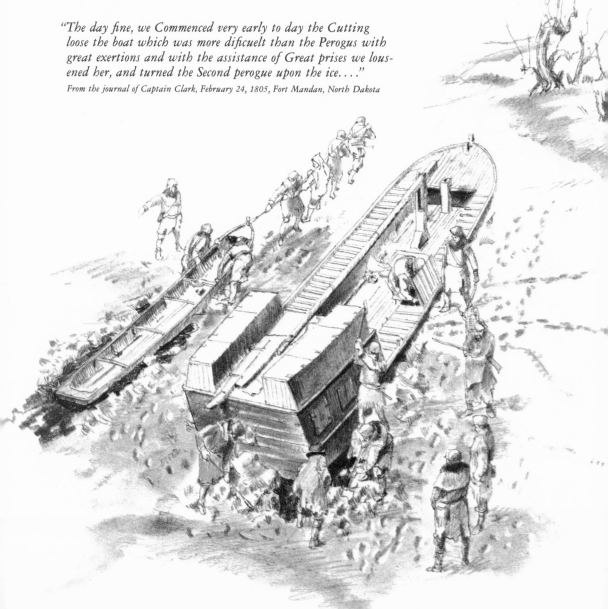

tains themselves, who, when they weren't serving as naturalists, geographers, geologists, engineers, and diplomats, had to act as doctors and surgeons. On January 27, 1805, Clark wrote: "Capt. Lewis took off the Toes of one foot of the Boy [an Indian] who got frost bit Some time ago." And four days later he recorded: "George Drewyer taken with the Pleurisy last evening Bled & gave him Some Sage tea, this morning he is much better."

On February 11 Sacagawea, heavy with her first child, began suffering severe labor pains. Clark was away on a hunting trip, and Lewis knew nothing of obstetrics. But a French-Canadian trader, René Jusseaume, who had been hired as an interpreter during the stay at the fort, had some advice for the captain. Jusseaume, who had lived among Indians for 15 years, told Lewis that in such cases he frequently administered a small portion of a powdered rattlesnake's rattle.

Lewis looked around, found a rattle, and gave it to Jusseaume. He carefully crushed two rings with his fingers and dropped the powder into a cup of water. This he gave to Sacagawea, and within 10 minutes she gave birth to "a fine boy."

"Whether this medicine was truly the cause or not," Lewis wrote, "I shall not undertake to determine."

Through much of February the men worked to free the keelboat and the two pirogues from the thick ice of the Missouri. When they chopped through one layer, water rushed in, making it virtually impossible to get at the layer beneath. They tried boiling water on hot stones to melt the ice, only to find that the rocks split into small pieces in the fire.

Finally, after days of chopping with axheads attached to long poles, the men were able to work the boats loose. Now the vessels could be pulled ashore and put in shape.

By early March, Clark could record at last, "A fine Day," for the thermometer stood at 40° *above* zero. With warmer weather came more Indians including, for the first time, the Hidatsa chief Le Borgne. As the chief arrived at the fort the morning of March 9 in the company of four other Indians, the captains set off a two-gun salute to greet him.

Le Borgne could not disguise his curiosity. In the course of conversation he disclosed that some foolish young men of his tribe had told him there was a *black* man among the explorers. The chief had seen white men many times before—traders from British posts in Canada as well as Frenchmen and Spaniards. But a man with black skin—this Le Borgne had neither seen nor heard of.

Lewis sent for York. With his good left eye, the unbelieving Hidatsa chief closely examined Clark's servant. Moistening his hand, he rubbed the Negro's skin to see if he wore paint.

Only when York took off his kerchief and showed his hair did Le Borgne believe that he had seen a black man.

As winter turned into spring, the expedition prepared to leave Fort Mandan. The men packed scores of items to be sent back to the President: skins of male and female pronghorns "with their Skelitons," a Mandan bow and a quiver of arrows, the bones of a coyote, tobacco seeds and an ear of corn, horns of mountain sheep, ceremonial buffalo robes, boxes of plants, cases containing a prairie dog, a sharp-tailed grouse, and four magpies, all alive, and dozens of "Sundery articles." With Clark's journal, kept since Wood River, Lewis sent a letter assuring Jefferson that "every individual of the party are in good health, and excellent sperits; zealously attached to the enterprise, and anxious to proceed; not a whisper of discontent or murmur is to be heard among them."

On April 7 the keelboat pushed south for St. Louis with Cpl. Richard Warfington in command. After an exchange of some French and Indian passengers at an Arikara village, the party would include an Arikara chief who had agreed to visit the President, two French traders, and six soldiers, including the two court-martialed men.

All through the winter the deserter Reed had remained indifferent, but the disgraced Newman had tried desperately to atone, once so over-exposing himself to the cold that his hands and feet had frozen. On recovering he had begged to continue with the expedition, but Lewis, fair but firm, refused, deeming it "impolitic to relax from the sentence, altho' he stood acquitted in my mind."

*T*HE SAME AFTERNOON Lewis and Clark and the main body of the expedition headed upriver once more — their vessels "not quite so rispectable as those of Columbus or Capt. Cook," Lewis admitted, but "still viewed by us with as much pleasure as those deservedly famed adventurers ever beheld theirs." The Corps of Discovery, in two large pirogues and six small canoes, now numbered 33, including "an Indian Woman wife to Charbono with a young child." Though Sacagawea spoke no English and would have to carry Jean Baptiste, her two-month-old infant, Lewis felt she was the expedition's "only dependence for a friendly negociation with the Snake [Shoshoni] Indians on whom we depend for horses to assist us in our portage from the Missouri to the columbia river."

While Clark took charge of the boats, Lewis rambled happily along the bank, obviously filled with pride: "we were now about to penetrate a country at least two thousand miles in width, on which the foot of civilized man had never trodden," he wrote; "the good or evil it had in store for us was for experiment yet to determine. . . . enterta[in]ing as I do, the most confident hope of succeeding in a voyage which had formed a da[r]ling project of mine for the last ten years, I could but esteem this moment of my departure as among the most happy of my life."

Nineteen days later the expedition reached the confluence of the Missouri and the Yellowstone Rivers, one of the great objectives of the journey. Lewis reported the men "much pleased at having arrived at this long wished for spot." The captains ordered drams of whiskey for all hands. Someone produced a fiddle, and the men spent the evening singing and dancing, for the moment unmindful of past trials and unconcerned about those yet to come.

Flat rock secures a buffalo skull atop a cairn; Assiniboin Indians erected the medicine sign to attract bison. Countless herds grazing across the prairies furnished Plains tribes the very substance for their way of life: food, shelter, tools, ornaments, and clothing.

BUFFALOES IN A FROZEN LAND

Shaggy buffaloes struggle through deep and drifting snow. Traveling across the plains, Lewis and Clark encountered bison by the thousand; today only scattered remnants remain of the huge herds that once ranged from Canada to Mexico, and from the Rocky Mountains to the Atlantic Ocean. Even cold weather brought little respite from hunters for the buffaloes' thick winter coats increased the value of their pelts. Plains Indians (above) chased herds from grazing grounds into snow-filled valleys; there the foundering bison fell victim to lances of snowshoed braves.

CHARLES M. RUSSELL, 1899, AMON CARTER MUSEUM, FORT WORTH (ABOVE); NORTHERN NATURAL GAS COMPANY COLLECTION, JOSLYN ART MUSEUM, OMAHA

TAKING ARMS AGAINST THE DARK HORDES

Buffaloes surge in panic over a precipice as warriors stampede the herd in a painting by Alfred Jacob Miller, who in 1837 became the first artist to travel into the Rockies. Many such jumps, called *pishkuns*, remained in use year after year; at the base of one, bones and debris covered five acres to a depth of several feet. Immediately after the drive, the Indians worked to exhaustion to butcher the kill and cut the meat into thin strips to dry. Although the chase — another way of hunting buffaloes — produced fewer kills, it required less organization and fewer participants. Quietly approaching a browsing herd, braves on horseback (left) lunged forward at a gallop, aiming their spears and arrows at a spot just behind the last rib of their prey. Later, as the Nation moved westward, sharpshooting white hunters began to take a heavy toll of the huge herds. In a single three-year span during the 1870's they slaughtered five million buffaloes, mainly for hides.

WINTER IN THE NORTH

Hidatsa Indian boys race across a patch of ice in a pole-and-hoop game. Their buffalo-robed elders watch intently; perhaps they have wagered on the outcome. In the background, women tend children near earth-and-timber lodges. Hidatsa Chief Black Moccasin (below), tottering from "more than a hundred snows" when Catlin painted him, asked after "Long Knife" and "Red Hair"—Lewis and Clark. Shortly before meeting the chief, the captains discovered the mule deer; its large ears reveal the aptness of the name they gave it.

WILLIAM ALBERT ALLARD

ABOUNDING WILDLIFE

Pronghorns dash across a snowy plain in a cream-and-buff blur; Clark admired them as "Keenly made and . . . butifull." The herd at left recalls his description of the animals' gait: "reather the rapid flight of birds than the motion of quadrupeds." Seldom able to approach within flintlock range of the swift, alert pronghorns, the men depended more on deer and elk for meat and skins. At right, a bull elk delivers a jab to the flank of a rival.

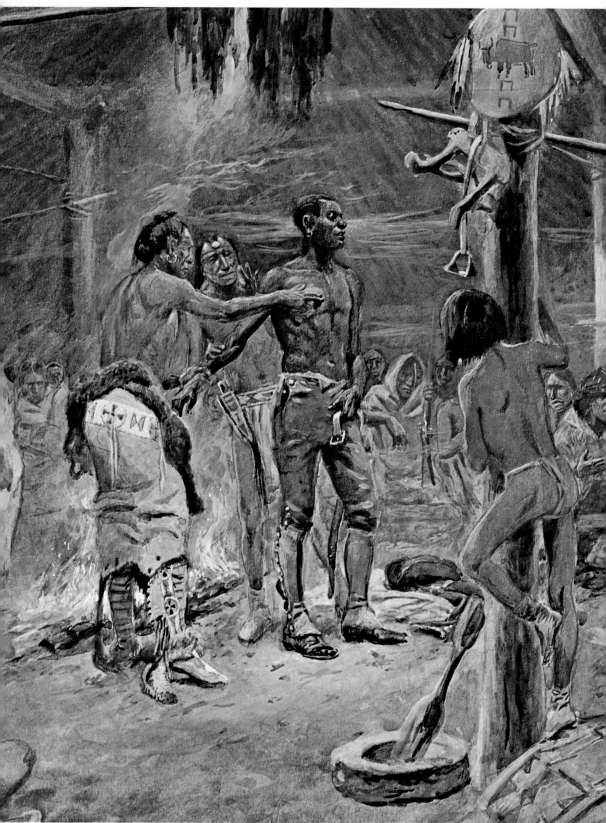

INDIANS MARVEL
AT A BLACK MAN

Suspecting a trick, Hidatsa Chief Le Borgne rubs moistened fingers across York's chest to see if he wears paint. The curious, one-eyed chief paid Lewis and Clark a call after his warriors reported that a black man accompanied the expedition. Captain Clark's slave enjoyed the commotion his color caused among Plains Indian tribes; once he pretended his master had captured him as a wild beast and tamed him. Farther to the west, though, Indians who had seen neither white nor black men made no distinction between them. Artist Russell modeled this scene after an earlier Bodmer view of a Mandan earth-lodge interior. Solidly built, such lodges formed the households of a settled and hospitable people. Light from the smokehole plays over a mortar for grinding corn, a bed of ornamented buffalo robes, and hunting gear. Through the winter Lewis and Clark often counciled with their Mandan and Hidatsa neighbors.

'THESE BEAR BEING SO HARD TO DIE REATHER INTIMEDATES US ALL'

GRIZZLY BEAR: SHOULDER HEIGHT 3–4′; WEIGHT 400–1,000 LBS.

Etched by the evening sun, a hump-shouldered grizzly pads beside a quiet creek. Largest American carnivores, these bears ruled the western prairies in the time of Lewis and Clark. After hairbreadth escapes from wounded, enraged grizzlies, Lewis concluded, "I . . . had reather fight two Indians than one bear." The explorers' records of bears taken, their range, and habits, eventually led to classing *Ursus horribilis* as a new species. He may seem as harmless as an overgrown teddy bear (below), but the grizzly's great strength and surprising speed command respect.

FRANK AND JOHN CRAIGHEAD

BEYOND THE YELLOWSTONE:
A TRUE WILDERNESS

Mountain-born rivers meet in western North Dakota farm country; the Yellow-stone empties into the darker, sediment-laden Missouri. In spring, as flights of wildfowl whistled overhead and the river rose, the explorers set forth from Fort Mandan "in excellent health and sperits" toward the confluence. Reaching the junction of the two rivers, Lewis and Clark marveled at the "wide and fertile val-lies." Game thronged the nearby plains. A salamander flickered in the grass, bees supped from evening primrose, and through it all trotted Scannon, Lewis's New-foundland dog, like the one at left. A proven member of the expedition, he hunted geese and rabbits for the camp pot; his watch kept curious grizzlies away.

Richard Scholes

Breaching the Wilderness

CHAPTER FIVE

BEYOND THE MOUTH of the Yellowstone, the explorers found a region swarming with wildlife. "Great numbers of Buffalow, Elk, Deer, antilope, beaver, Porcupins, & water fowls seen to day," wrote Clark on the first Friday of May 1805 as the boats turned their prows into a land that would become known as the Big Sky Country of Montana.

Driving with my family out of the Dakotas, bound for a voyage up a twisting wilderness corridor of the Missouri, I compared notes with Lewis. The raw landscape seemed just as he had found it — "beautifull as far as the eye can reach.... beatifull in the extreme." Gone were the buffaloes, the countless herds of elk and deer, and the bands of racing antelope. But the great, open stretches of land, the uncluttered fields, the appearance of an eternal emptiness remained.

"It's almost the way God created it," intoned a proud Montanan we met one day. "As far as the eye can see there's not a town. This is the fourth-largest state in the Union, and we only have 700,000 people. That mountain there, it must be 75 miles away. You could cross it and travel for two or three days and not meet another human being. It's good to know that there still are places like this left in the United States."

Into that open, unspoiled land we now drove, eager to rendezvous with our boat. Ahead, deep in the hills of north-central Montana, flowed a 155-mile stretch of the Missouri little changed since the days of Lewis and

"...Saw a large brown bear.... he took the River and was near catching the Man he chased in, but he went up against the Stream and the bear being wounded could not git to him. one of the hunters Shot him in the head...."
From the journal of Sergeant Ordway, May 14, 1805, near the mouth of the Musselshell River in Montana.
Drawing of bighorn sheep (above) by Captain Clark; Missouri Historical Society.

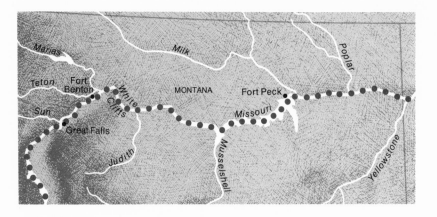

Leaving the junction of the Missouri and Yellowstone Rivers, the expedition pushed into the heart of the wilderness. The party encountered fierce grizzlies, and the white pirogue almost capsized. Passing through the White Cliffs of modern-day Montana, the men reached the Great Falls of the Missouri and prepared to portage the cataracts.

Clark. There by boat they had traveled, and there by boat we would go, pitching our tents where they had pitched theirs, sharing in the wonders of a primitive world.

This promise before us, we kept close to the river as it poured from the west, sometimes pausing to let sheep stroll across our path, sometimes to watch the children fish, to sniff the scent of wild roses that grew by the roadside, or to listen to the sound of the river as it gurgled peacefully around the branches of partially submerged trees. As we traveled we talked of the buckskin-clad explorers, rowing and poling and hauling their boats deeper and deeper into the wilderness — and into a country populated by ferocious bears.

On April 29, Lewis and another hunter found and wounded two of these creatures, the first they had seen of the breed. Suddenly one of the bears charged toward the captain. Lewis turned, and for 70 or 80 yards they ran, man and beast, until at last the captain was able to pause to reload his rifle and help kill the lumbering animal. "It was a male not fully grown...300 lbs....The legs of this bear are somewhat longer than those of the black, as are it's tallons and tusks incomparably larger and longer....it's colour is yellowish brown, the eyes small, black, and piercing; the front of the fore legs near the feet is usually black; the fur is finer thicker and deeper than that of the black bear."

Not until 1815 would these huge creatures be declared a separate species, but here was the first detailed anatomical description of the monarch of North American carnivores — *Ursus horribilis,* the great grizzly.

Less than a week later the explorers killed a full-grown male weighing some 600 pounds and measuring 8 feet 7½ inches in height and 5 feet 10½ inches in girth. It took 10 shots to bring him down.

Despite the encounters, Lewis still felt confidently superior to the beasts: "the Indians may well fear this anamal equiped as they generally are with their bows and arrows...but in the hands of skillfull riflemen," he boasted, "they are by no means as formidable or dangerous as they have been represented."

The next grizzly he met gave him pause to reflect on his words. Sailing on — "the courant strong," the river "very crooked," Lewis recalled — the explorers were surprised one day by the sight of Bratton running toward the boats, frightened and out of breath. He had been chased by a wounded bear. Immediately Lewis set out through the brush with seven of the party "in quest of this monster."

For a mile they followed the trail of the grizzly's blood. Finally they found him still "perfectly alive." Although shot through the lungs by Bratton, the mighty creature had summoned the strength to dig a bed in the earth about two feet deep and five feet long. It took two more balls through the skull to kill him.

Lewis now had to admit that he did not like these "gentlemen" after all. He would rather fight "two Indians than one bear."

The name given to the scene of one such incident—Yellow Bear Defeat Creek—soon would be forgotten. But the near-tragic event that followed on May 14 long would be remembered. Lewis, for one, would look back on the day with "utmost trepidation and horror."

Both Lewis and Clark had left the boats to walk along the bank, something they rarely did together. A sudden squall began to kick up the river. A violent gust struck the white pirogue. At the helm sat Sacagawea's husband Charbonneau, the one man least qualified to cope with the situation. The vessel contained the expedition's papers, books, instruments, medicine, and "almost every article indispensibly necessary to . . . insure the success of the enterprize," as Lewis later summarized.

Helplessly, Lewis and Clark stood by as Charbonneau, "perhaps the most timid waterman in the world," did precisely the wrong thing. Instead of putting the pirogue before the wind, he "lufted her up into it," Lewis wrote. When the wind forced the sail's brace out of the hands of the man handling it, the boat turned on its side. It would have gone "completely topsaturva" had not the vessel's awning resisted the wind.

*I*N DESPERATION the captains fired their rifles into the air. Lewis threw down his weapon and pouch and began to unbutton his coat. He would swim through the high waves and cold current—a plan so futile, he realized in time, that had he attempted it, he "should have paid the forfit of my life."

Instead he stood with Clark shouting orders: Cut the halyards. Haul in the sail. In the confusion no one heard, and the pirogue lay on her side, taking in water for a full 30 seconds before someone finally pulled in the sail. Even as the boat miraculously righted itself, Charbonneau cried out hysterically, dropping the tiller and begging God for mercy.

At the bow Cruzatte raged. He threatened to shoot Charbonneau instantly if he did not take hold of the rudder. At last Charbonneau did, and while some of the men bailed frantically with kettles, Cruzatte and two others rowed the pirogue ashore.

Calmest of all was Sacagawea. In water up to her waist—and holding her papoose through it all—she had kept her head, gathering into the pirogue everything that she could of the supplies and equipment that had been swept overboard.

As far as Lewis was concerned, she stood in "equal fortitude and resolution, with any person onboard at the time of the accedent."

The next day the men spread the articles out to dry, and Whitehouse
observed: "the Medicine Spoiled or damaged very much Some of the
paper and nearly all the books got wet."

Might not one book, Lewis's journal for the first leg of the voyage —
if he did keep one regularly — have been lost to the swift waters of the
Missouri? At least one historian who has done extensive research on the
papers of Lewis and Clark, Dr. Donald Jackson of the University of
Virginia, is intrigued by the thought. Such an incident might explain why
no Lewis journal, except for occasional fragments, exists for the period
prior to March 1805.

Our rendezvous with the implacable Missouri was close at hand. At
Montana's Kipp State Park we met the crew of the boat I had hired
several weeks before.

Traveling upstream posed an interesting challenge to the Upper Missouri Wilderness Waterway Cruise Company. "Normally we float downstream and trail our boats back upriver to Fort Benton," our crewmaster
Bill Kindzerski explained as we put aboard with our gear, "so this will
be a good test for us." The boat's pilot, Bob Singer, started the 65-horse-
power outboard. Soon the 20-foot open-decked barge was on its way,
carrying us on a five-day journey through the wilderness.

Past wild flowers that bloomed at the water's edge and beneath puffy
cottonwood seeds that drifted airily overhead, Bob wove a course familiar
from years of navigating the river. He skirted hidden sandbars and snags
that he knew lay beneath the choppy, wind-whipped waves and riffles.
"The law of averages says the current is on the outside of the bend," he
explained, "but on the Missouri this is not necessarily so."

Hardly an hour had passed when we spied on the face of a high, almost
perpendicular, bluff the graceful forms of mountain sheep. Like silent
emissaries out of the adventure of Lewis and Clark, they looked at us
curiously, motionless, every head pointed our way, their horns "compressed, bent backwards...swelling into wavey rings," just as Clark had
written of the same bighorn species the expedition had seen.

We felt gratified to learn that the Montana Fish and Game Commission
had chosen to reintroduce the animals into the area.

It must have been amid scenes like this that on Sunday, May 26, Lewis
—alone except for Scannon—climbed a high hill and in the distance beheld what he thought were a few snow-covered points of the Rocky
Mountains. Bathed in sunlight, the peaks glistened as brightly as the
captain's expectations.

"I felt a secret pleasure," he wrote rhapsodically, "in finding myself
so near the head of the heretofore conceived boundless Missouri."

What suffering and hardship these peaks would impose on his men.
Thinking about this, he felt his joy "counterballanced." But, he reflected,
"as I have always held it a crime to anticipate evils I will believe it a good
comfortable road untill I am compelled to believe differently."

The same day Lewis killed a buffalo and a rattlesnake, and saw elk and bighorns and "several softshelled Turtles which were the first that have been seen this season." The land itself remained bare and rocky, with hardly any timber except the scattered clumps of pine and spruce that crowned the dry heights.

"This is truly a desert barren country," he wrote, in words that I myself might have chosen as our little boat churned up the broad stream. The civilized world slid far behind us; the only signs of man we saw were the scattered herds of ranchers' cattle, a few dirt roads and ferry crossings, and occasionally the crumbled cabin of a "wood hawk" who once had sold firewood to sternwheel steamers that ventured upriver before the coming of the railroad in the 1880's.

As we sailed deeper into the wilderness, into the "high broken [and] rockey" country that Ordway described, Danny caught sight of a golden

"...Perogue was under sail when a sudon squawl of wind struck her obliquely, and turned her considerably ...Charbono still crying to his god for mercy, had not yet recollected the rudder....the Indian woman ... caught and preserved most of the light articles which were washed overboard."

From the journal of Captain Lewis, May 14 and 16, 1805, near the mouth of the Musselshell

eagle, and we all watched it soar over the top of a high precipice. On the walls of the steep bluff itself tiny cliff swallows fluttered in and out of bulb-shaped nests they had built of mud.

"Did Lewis and Clark see those?" Michele asked.

"Yes, and those too," I told her, pointing to two birds that flew low over the water. Their white "chin straps" and black heads and necks identified them as Canada geese, which Lewis and Clark had seen by the thousand.

Then suddenly among the cliffs there appeared what struck me as nature's way of hinting at strange things to come. The wind and rain of centuries had eroded the sandstone outcroppings into umbrella-like shapes with capstones of hard rock sitting on stems of softer stone.

"They look to me like mushrooms," Michele said, quite accurately.

In the afternoon the sky darkened, and black clouds scowled down at the lonely hills. A sudden gust carried Arlette's hat with it. We turned around, and Bill fished the wet straw out of the water with a pole he was using to measure the river's depth. As we turned toward land to break out raingear, he sounded a deepening channel: "a foot . . . a foot and a half . . . two feet plus . . . three feet."

" 'Scarcely any bottoms to the river,' " I could hardly resist commenting, quoting words that Lewis had used on this same stretch of water.

*T*HAT NIGHT we pitched our tents in the rain on a low cotton-wood plain. After a dinner of steak and potatoes, we turned in, listening—snug in our sleeping bags—to the rush of the wind through the lofty trees and the beat of the rain on our tent. Outside, on the netting of our entrance flap, I could see long-legged mosquitoes pointing our way.

As the rain subsided, I drifted off to sleep to the trill of a thrush lifting its plaintive song across the silent, lonely hills.

Through all of our second day we traveled in a cold rain that slashed across our faces. Trying to keep dry, Arlette and the children huddled together under a protective sheet of black polyethylene we had taken along for just such a circumstance.

As our boat bounced and lurched through a series of rapids, foamy white waves churned up over hidden rocks, warning us to keep our distance. Beyond the rapids we sped forward at full throttle past hills streaked with beds of impure coal.

"Near there Lewis and Clark camped on the night of May 28, 1805," Bob said, pointing toward a level area crowded with islands. In the darkness of that night a buffalo bull had stumbled onto the expedition's white pirogue and blundered wildly through camp, just missing by inches the heads of a group of sleeping men.

As the beast charged toward the captains' tent, Scannon jumped out and barked, and the bull changed its course and bounded off into the night, leaving the men "in an uproar with our guns in o[u]r hands," explained Lewis. If the buffalo had "trod on a man," Ordway wrote, "it would have killed him dead."

The white pirogue again. To Lewis it seemed as if the vessel were "attended by some evil gennii." Clark chose to dwell on more pleasant thoughts. Passing the mouth of a stream that flowed into the Missouri from the south, he named it Judith River, after a girl back in Virginia. Julia Hancock—or Judy as her friends called her—was only 13 years old at the time, but one day she would marry the explorer.

About a mile above the Judith we camped in the rain once more, but the next day the weather began to clear. As great patches of blue showed through the dark clouds we took the journals in hand and went looking for a place Lewis mentioned in his diary. On May 29, 1805, he wrote: "today we passed on the Stard. side the remains of a vast many mangled carcases of Buffalow which had been driven over a precipice of 120 feet by the Indians and perished."

A warrior would disguise himself in a buffalo robe and then place himself strategically between the herd and the precipice. At a signal other Indians would appear behind the buffaloes, and the frightened animals would stampede in the direction of the decoy—only to plunge to their deaths over the cliff.

"What happened to the warrior?" Michele wanted to know.

For the answer to her question I had only to turn again to Lewis's journal: If those who play the part of the decoy "are not very fleet runers the buffaloe tread them under foot and crush them to death, and sometimes drive them over the precipice also, where they perish in common with the buffaloe."

In some places along the river, layers of bones still mark the sites of these buffalo jumps, but no one has found the place mentioned by Lewis; apparently the river long ago washed away the evidence.

Where Lewis and Clark had stopped the evening of May 29, we put in for lunch. As I strolled along the bank alone, listening to the quiet murmur of the wind through the cottonwood trees, I felt a strong affinity with those weary explorers who had camped and fixed their fire on this same "point of woodland."

A little farther upriver we left the boats and crept quietly to a level, treeless plain to eavesdrop on a colony of curious animals standing up on their hind legs and making sounds like the "Whisteling noise" Clark had heard such creatures make. The chirping soon stopped as the restless little rodents slipped into their dark subterranean passageways.

Before we left I took time to explain to the children that Lewis and Clark had been the first to describe these animals, and that Ordway may have been the first to give them the name by which we know them today —prairie dogs.

Beyond the next rapids the scenery suddenly began to change. The cliffs blossomed with stone "toadstools" of extraordinary shapes. During much of the next two days, for about 30 miles, the land itself entertained us as it had nowhere else on the Missouri.

Rocky outcroppings, honed by wind and water over thousands of years, rose high and bold from the banks. All around us glistened the

turrets, the cupolas, the spires, the arches of a white, enchanted world limited only by the confines of our imaginations. From many a fancied minaret, I could almost hear the sad wail of the muezzin summoning the faithful to prayer.

"There!" Arlette pointed. "That looks like the ruins of a whole city, with crumbling buildings and bridges and walls."

"Do people live there?" little Danny asked, springing to a better position in the boat.

"I'll bet they could," Michele responded, as though at any moment she expected a drawbridge to lower before a castle in the distance. If a knight on a white charger suddenly had appeared, I doubt that she would have been surprised.

In eerie contrast to all the whiteness, black shonkinite domes thrust out of the earth at many points, and igneous dikes, following along fault planes, formed walls of stones so perfectly placed it seemed that they had been put together by the hand of man.

A similar thought had struck Lewis as he traveled this great sweep of the river now called the White Cliffs. "I should have thought that nature had attempted here to rival the human art of masonry had I not recollected that she first began her work," he wrote.

The passing years seemed to have done nothing to lessen the visual impact of these great cliffs.

The "thousand grotesque figures," the "lofty freestone buildings," their parapets "well stocked with statuary," the "ruins of eligant buildings,"

"...a large buffaloe Bull...ran up the bank in full speed ...within a few inches of the heads of one range of the men as they yet lay sleeping...my dog saved us by causing him to change his course...."

From the journal of Captain Lewis, May 29, 1805, near the mouth of the Judith River

with their columns, pedestals, and capitals that had so entranced the explorers on May 31 had no less an effect on us. "As we passed on," Lewis wrote, "it seemed as if those seens of visionary inchantment would never...end."

Today there is talk that someday buffaloes, bighorns, bald eagles, cougars, wolves, wolverines, and many other once-native species of wildlife will be reintroduced in abundance along this remote stretch of the Missouri River. The Department of the Interior has proposed designating a 100-mile-long area as the Missouri Breaks National River "to safeguard for all time, undammed and unspoiled," this wilderness monument to Lewis and Clark.

But another plan calls for building a dam to provide electric power and water for irrigation.

The thought of the alternative made us sad.

Late on the fourth day of our river journey we arrived at a point where the Missouri reached out in two directions. In the glow of our fire we pitched our tents "on the Lard. Side at the forks of the river," where the expedition had camped on June 2, 1805.

In what must have been the understatement of the entire journey so far, Lewis wrote that an "interesting question" was now to be determined: Which of these rivers was the Missouri?

Which way the dream of Lewis and Clark and Thomas Jefferson?

Which way to the Pacific?

Two months of the traveling season already had elapsed. Lewis well understood that a time-consuming mistake "would probably so dishearten the party that it might defeat the expedition altogether."

Lewis and Clark took no chances. They decided to delay while two canoes with three men each traveled the streams to learn their widths, their depths, and their currents. Gass led one party up the river which flowed from the south, and Pryor took the other group up the river which ran from the north.

Returning that evening, Gass reported that the south branch was clear and rapid and contained a great many islands. The north branch, Pryor had learned, was muddy and less rapid, and comparatively shallow. But the question of which was the true Missouri remained unsettled.

The captains would have to find out for themselves. With five men, Clark traveled 40 miles up the south fork, while Lewis and six men followed the north fork. Clark returned after two days without mishap, but Lewis proved less lucky.

At the top of a 90-foot precipice made treacherous by rain, he slipped and fell. He barely saved himself by driving his spontoon into the ground. Then, as he got to his feet, a voice behind him cried out.

Lewis turned and saw Pvt. Richard Windsor hanging over the cliff, holding on with his left arm and leg. It appeared as if he might lose his tenuous grip at any instant.

Calmly, so as not to alarm the private further, Lewis assured him he was in no danger.

Use your right hand, he told Windsor. Take your knife from your belt. Now dig a toehold for your right foot in the side of the cliff. Slowly, assured by Lewis's calmness, Windsor rose to his knees.

Now slip off the moccasins, Lewis told him. Take your rifle in one hand, your knife in the other, and crawl forward on hands and knees. And finally, Windsor reached safety.

At the end of the day Lewis lay down to rest on some willow boughs. He felt "fully repaid for the toil and pain of the day, so much will a good shelter, a dry bed, and comfortable supper revive the sperits of the w[e]aryed, wet and hungry traveler."

Independently, the two captains had arrived at the same conclusion: The south branch was the true Missouri. Lewis felt sure that the other river "had it's direction too much to the North for our rout to the Pacific." But when Lewis and Clark returned to camp, they found that the whole party to a man felt that the north branch, and not the south, was the right river. After all, the men reasoned, wasn't the north fork brown and muddy like the river they had been on for so long.

"Why didn't Sacagawea just tell them which was the right way?" Michele asked me as we stood at the confluence of the two rivers. "Wasn't she their guide?"

"No, she wasn't really," I replied, "although many people have grown up thinking that she was. She didn't tell them which was the true Missouri because she simply didn't know."

Since doubt remained about which was the right river, the captains decided that Lewis would take four men and follow the south branch on foot in search of the one unmistakable sign of the true Missouri—the great waterfalls that Indians had told them about at Fort Mandan. While Lewis was gone, Clark would remain at the confluence to lighten the burden of the hard voyage to come by caching the red pirogue and about 1,000 pounds of clothing, ammunition, equipment, and food for use on the return trip.

With a touch of chivalry Lewis named the north branch Maria's River, in honor of his cousin Maria Wood. The muddy turbulent waters "but illy comport with the pure celestial virtues and amiable qualifications of that lovely fair one," he wrote, "but on the other hand it is a noble river."

For a number of days Lewis had been sick with dysentery. Shortly after his departure he began suffering violent pains and soon developed a high fever. Toward evening, as the pain worsened, he did what his mother Lucy would have done back in Albemarle County—he resolved "to try an experiment with some simples."

Lucy would have been proud. Looking around, Lewis found some chokecherry shrubs. He had his men gather some of them and watched as they stripped off the leaves, cut the twigs into pieces two inches long, and boiled them in water "untill a strong black decoction of an astringent bitter tast was produced."

At sunset Lewis drank a pint of the brew and about an hour later repeated the dose; "by 10 in the evening," he wrote, "I was entirely

relieved from pain and in fact every symptom of the disorder forsook me; my fever abated, a gentle perspiration was produced and I had a comfortable and refreshing nights rest."

Two days later, on Thursday, June 13, the captain found what he had been looking for. Hearing the distant sound of falling water, he advanced to see a spray "arrise above the plain like a collumn of smoke," accompanied by "a roaring too tremendious to be mistaken for any cause short of the great falls." There could be no doubt. The south fork had a name. It was the Missouri.

Impatiently, Lewis hurried down a hill, and from a ledge of rocks he stared in astonishment. Cascading over bluffs some 300 yards wide and about 80 feet high, the water beat furiously, foaming and frothing. He stood motionless, yearning for the gift of writing or drawing "to give to the enlightened world some just idea of this truly magnificent and sublimely grand object, which has from the commencement of time been concealed from the view of civilized man."

At sunrise the next morning Lewis dispatched Joseph Field with a letter

"...I heard a voice behind me cry out god god Capt. what shall I do...I found it was Windsor who had sliped and fallen...his wright hand arm and leg over the precipice while he was holding on with the left arm and foot....I expected every instant to see him loose his strength and slip off...."

From the journal of Captain Lewis, June 7, 1805, on the Marias River

to Clark bearing news of the great discovery. While Clark pushed up the Missouri, Lewis continued to explore, finding a series of rapids and four smaller waterfalls, each seeming to rival the others in glory.

Leaving our boat at Fort Benton, we drove southwestward toward the goal Lewis had sought. But we found little of the "grand specticle" that he had seen.

Today little of the glory remains. Hydroelectric projects near the city of Great Falls blanket the sites. Colter Falls lies completely lost under a dam's quiet pool, and each of the others is surmounted by dams.

After discovering the falls Lewis "thought it would be well to kill a buffaloe" for food, and from a herd of at least a thousand, he picked out a fat specimen "and shot him very well." While waiting for the animal to fall, he turned to discover a grizzly stealing toward him.

*I*NSTANTLY Lewis raised his rifle, only to realize it wasn't loaded. By now the bear was charging, and Lewis knew that the only thing to do was flee. For about 80 yards they ran, the grizzly gaining with every step.

When at last Lewis reached the river, he plunged in up to his waist, and whipped around, preparing to battle the animal with his spontoon. Then, with "quite as great precipitation as he had just before pursued me," the bear retreated.

"I felt myself not a little gratifyed that he had declined the combat," the captain later recounted, vowing never again to "suffer my peice to be longer empty than the time she necessarily required to charge her."

Catching up with Lewis, Clark brought grave news: Sacagawea was feverish, her pulse slight and irregular. Clark had done all he could; he had bled her and given her a "doste of salts" and applied a poultice of bark to her abdomen, but the pains persisted. Lewis continued the treatment. He was concerned "for the poor object herself," of course, but also for her being "our only dependence for a friendly negociation with the . . . Indians on whom we depend for horses to assist us in our portage from the Missouri to the columbia river."

Lewis ordered water brought from a nearby sulphur spring, "the virtues of which," he "now resolved to try on the Indian woman." Almost miraculously, the mineral water did its work. Sacagawea's pulse became regular, and soon she was eating broiled buffalo "and rich soope of the same meat."

If one problem seemed solved, another was just to begin, for ahead lay an obstacle greater than any the explorers had encountered thus far in their journey—the awesome Great Falls of the Missouri. While Clark set out to examine the country for the best possible overland route around the falls, Lewis set six men to work making wheels and axles and tongues for the crude wagons they would use to haul the canoes and supplies.

"We . . . are about to enter on the most perilous and dificuelt part of our Voyage," wrote Clark, yet "all appear ready to meet thos dificuelties which await us with resolution and becomeing fortitude."

Spyglass in hand, Lewis gains his first view of the Rocky Mountains — possibly the Sawtooth Range of western Montana. Climbing to this jagged summit on May 26, 1805, he "felt a secret pleasure in finding myself so near the head of the heretofore conceived boundless Missouri."

'SEENS OF VISIONARY INCHANTMENT'

Bathed by a Montana sunset, the White Cliffs of the Missouri River loom above a primitive wilderness region largely untouched by encroaching civilization. The sandstone bluffs, rising to heights of 300 feet, made a deep impression on Lewis. With the "help of a little imagination and an oblique view," he wrote on May 31, 1805, the hills "at a distance are made to represent eligant ranges of lofty freestone buildings.... it seemed as if those seens of visionary inchantment would never have and end." Countering proposals for a high dam that would inundate much of the scenic area, the National Park Service hopes to preserve a 100-mile-long segment of free-flowing water as the Missouri Breaks National River.

'STOCKED WITH STATUARY'

Sculpted by centuries of wind and rain, rocky sentinels painted by Bodmer (opposite) recall Lewis's description of "parapets . . . stocked with statuary." While the artist worked, a herd of bighorn sheep grazed on nearby hills. On a Missouri River sandbank, Bodmer portrayed a hunter from Maximilian's party (above) stalking a ravenous grizzly found feeding on a buffalo carcass. Indians erected the pyramid of elk horns (below) as a charm to bring success in hunting.

KARL BODMER 1833, COLLECTION OF MR. AND MRS. PAUL MELLON

TO THE GREAT FALLS AND BEYOND

Echoing the "tremendious roaring" that greeted Lewis on June 14, 1805, Montana's Rainbow Falls descends and "rises into foaming billows of great hight ... hising flashing and sparkling as it departs." For two backbreaking weeks, the expedition portaged this fall and four others near today's city of Great Falls. Dams now crown four of the falls, and water covers another. In the Big Belt Mountains two weeks later, the party sailed through a rock-ribbed gorge (opposite far left) that Lewis called the Gates of the Rocky Mountains. At left mushroom-shaped outcroppings poke from eroded cliffs that earlier awed the explorers.

Richard Schlecht

The Cruel Mountains

CHAPTER SIX

ON JUNE 21 the great portage began. Eighteen miles had marked a fair day's travel on the Missouri, but it took two weeks to cover the same distance around the falls. In searing heat the explorers struggled up steep slopes and around gullies, over rocks and prickly pears, as they pushed and pulled and dragged and carried the heavy canoes.

Wrote Clark: "the men has to haul with all their strength wate & art." The buffalo-trampled earth had dried into sharp points that pierced the soles of their moccasins. Many limped, and some fainted. Yet no one complained; "all go with cheerfullness," reported Lewis. During one pause those still "able to shake a foot" square danced to the music of Cruzatte's fiddle. And once they had reached more-level terrain, some wizard among the group got the idea of hoisting sails on the dugout-laden wagons to make hauling easier.

Reaching the Missouri again, the men rested and prepared to resume their river journey. At last Lewis could launch his iron-frame boat, the *Experiment,* which had been carried all the way from Harper's Ferry for just such an occasion; it would take the place of the white pirogue that had been cached before the expedition portaged the falls.

Eagerly the captain directed the assembling of the sections of the 36-foot-long framework. Over it the men stretched buffalo and elk hides. Unable to obtain sufficient pitch with which to caulk the seams of the

"...the sales were hois[t]ed in the Canoes as the men were drawing them and the wind was great relief to them being sufficiently strong to move the canoes on the Trucks, this is Saleing on Dry land in every sence of the word...."
From the journal of Captain Clark, June 25, 1805, as the expedition portaged the Great Falls of the Missouri. Sketch of Shoshoni pipe (above) by Captain Lewis; American Philosophical Society, Philadelphia.

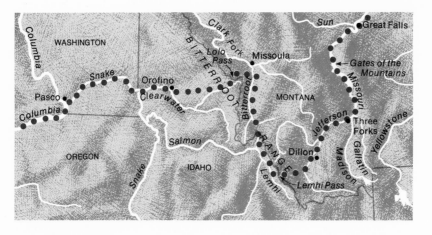

After portaging its Great Falls, the explorers continued up the Missouri into the Rockies where they obtained horses from the Indians. In a struggle against hunger, cold, and exhaustion, they crossed the Bitterroot Range. Stopping to make dugouts beside the Clearwater, the voyagers traveled to the Columbia via the Snake River.

vessel, they prepared a substitute, using a mixture of pounded charcoal, beeswax, and buffalo tallow.

Once launched, the boat floated "like a perfect cork," Lewis noted, but not for long. Soon the pitch substitute started to crack and peel, and the boat began to leak. The *Experiment* had failed, a circumstance that "mortifyed me not a little," the captain recounted. He ordered the frame stripped of its covering, and the men set about preparing two new dugouts.

On July 15 the expedition started upstream once more, and in their footsteps we followed, first by car through low, rolling hills, and then by boat. Boarding the motor launch *Sacajawea,* we joined a boatload of tourists traveling through an area of "remarkable clifts" that Lewis had reported seeing on July 19, 1805.

Lewis marveled at the view: "every object here wears a dark and gloomy aspect. . . . the river appears to have forced it's way through this immence body of solid rock for the distance of 5¾ Miles and where it makes it's exit below has th[r]own on either side vast collumns of rocks mountains high. . . . from the singular appearance of this place I called it the *gates of the rocky mounatains.*" "Gates of the Mountains" it is called today.

On the 20th Lewis saw in the distance what could be a real sign of Indians. Smoke rose from the plains, possibly one party signaling another that strange men were sailing upriver. Everyone wondered: Could they be nearing the land of the Shoshonis—Sacagawea's people— from whom Lewis and Clark hoped to obtain the horses they would need to traverse the mountains ahead?

Two days later Sacagawea suddenly began to recognize the country; this was the river "on which her relations live," she told Lewis. Traveling ahead of the main party, Clark reached the Three Forks of the Missouri. Eager to find the Shoshonis, he headed up the west fork, rejoining the main party two days later. Still no Shoshonis.

The explorers grew anxious: "if we do not find them or some other nation who have horses I fear the successfull issue of our voyage will be very doubtfull," Lewis wrote. "We are now several hundred miles within the bosom of this wild and mountanous country . . . without any information with rispect to the country not knowing how far these mountains continue, or wher to direct our course to pass them to advantage or intersept a navigable branch of the Columbia."

Before setting off, Lewis and Clark chose names for each of the forks. The west fork, the one they would travel, they called the Jefferson "in honor of that illustrious personage Thomas Jefferson." They named the middle fork the Madison for Secretary of State James Madison, and the east fork the Gallatin for Secretary of the Treasury Albert Gallatin.

The voyagers struggled up the Jefferson, hauling their boats through the rapids. Many of the men came up lame, one suffered a dislocated arm, and Gass strained his back. So "fortiegued" had everyone become, wrote Lewis, they wished only "that navigation was at an end that they might go by land."

The one woman among them gave them new hope. Sacagawea spotted a hill that she thought resembled the head of a beaver. Just across the mountains to the west lay the summer retreat of her people.

The hill Sacagawea recognized rises 13 miles south of the town of Twin Bridges, Montana, near where the Big Hole and Beaverhead Rivers join to form the Jefferson. As we drove near a long series of rolling hills that ended abruptly in the knobby eminence, excitement quickly spread through our little group. The mere suggestion of a beaver had made it look like one to the children. Michele could see its mouth and ears and Danny its "big flat tail." But, like Sacagawea, they were mistaken. The hill, known locally today as Point of Rocks, stands 20 miles north of the point now identified as the true "beaver's head."

"So Sacagawea must have confused the two," Arlette reasoned.

But the Bird Woman's words had encouraged the men. Lewis took Drouillard, Shields, and Pvt. Hugh McNeal and set out overland, resolved to find some Indians "if it should cause me a trip of one month."

*T*HE FOUR followed an old Indian trail and then a creek that flowed from the west. Suddenly, Lewis saw a faint shape coming down the plain. He raised his telescope, and the vague figure, about two miles distant, took form. It was a horseman, the first Indian any member of the expedition had seen since leaving the land of the Mandans and Hidatsas in mid-April.

Feeling sure the rider was a Shoshoni, Lewis edged forward. When they came within about a mile of each other, the Indian halted, and Lewis took a blanket from his knapsack; in an Indian sign of friendship he held the cloth at two corners and waved it in the air as if "spreading a robe or skin for ther gests to set on when they are visited." He made the gesture three times, but it did not have "the desired effect."

Taking some beads, a mirror, and a few trinkets, he moved, unarmed, to within 200 paces of the horseman, who still stared suspiciously, as though afraid, Lewis thought, "of our having some unfriendly design upon him."

"Tab-ba-bone...tab-ba-bone," Lewis yelled as loudly as he could. The captain had not learned his Shoshoni well. Instead of identifying himself

as "White Man...white man," which in Shoshoni is *"Tai-va-vone...
tai-va-vone,"* he was calling out, "Stranger...alien."

The Indian began backing off. And when Shields unwittingly pressed forward too quickly, the frightened scout wheeled his horse and galloped away. With him, Lewis wrote, went "all my hopes of obtaining horses for the preasent."

Into the region of Lewis's abortive confrontation we traveled, bumping over a narrow dirt road. With us was a group of Lewis and Clark buffs from Dillon, Montana—among them our guide, Wally Gallaher, supervisor of Beaverhead National Forest, and Mrs. Fred Woodside of the Beaverhead Museum Association.

We stopped high in the hills, and while the children picked flowers, Arlette and I dipped our hands into the same clear brook that had refreshed the advance party of the Corps of Discovery on August 12, 1805. Lewis wrote that Private McNeal had "exultingly stood with a foot on each side of this little rivulet and thanked his god that he had lived to bestride the mighty & heretofore deemed endless Missouri."

Not far ahead Lewis discovered the source of the stream, a spring that gushed from the soggy earth. Here, near a grove of Douglas firs and lodgepole pines—some of the firs two centuries old—I knelt and tasted the "pure and ice-cold" water, as Lewis had done.

Lewis thought he had reached "the most distant fountain of the waters of the mighty Missouri.... one of those great objects on which my mind has been unalterably fixed for many years." But he was mistaken. The distant fountain flows to the east at the head of the Red Rock River, another branch of the Beaverhead.

Beyond the summit of Lemhi Pass—where a wooden fence today skips and hops along the ridges of the Continental Divide, the western boundary of the Louisiana Purchase—Lewis made another miscalculation. Hiking into what is now Idaho, he found a westward-flowing "handsome bold running Creek" that he took to be the Columbia. Though part of the Columbia River watershed, the stream is actually a tributary of the Lemhi River. But it led the explorers to the Shoshonis.

Moving through the valley the next day, Lewis spotted three Indians —two women and a man—but they fled when he approached. His next encounter brought him better luck. Only one of a group of three women fled, and she soon returned. Lewis distributed gifts and painted the tawny cheeks of all three "with some vermillion which with this nation is emblematic of peace."

Only two miles farther on, the women now guiding, Lewis met 60 Shoshoni warriors "mounted on excellent horses, who came in nearly full speed."

The women "exultingly shewed the presents," and the Shoshonis soon were embracing the captain affectionately to cries of *"âh-hí-e! âh-hí-e!"* — "I am much pleased, I am much rejoiced."

Cameahwait, their chief, threw his arm over Lewis's shoulder and pressed his cheek to the captain's. The braves joined in, and "we wer all carressed and besmeared with their grease and paint till I was heartily tired of the national hug," the captain recounted.

For a day the explorers rested, and as they smoked the peace pipe with the Shoshonis, Lewis explained the white men's mission. Then Lewis and his men set out with Cameahwait to meet Clark and, he hoped, to trade for some of the 400 horses which Drouillard had noticed were feeding around the Indian camp.

On August 17 Drouillard and several Indians riding in advance of Lewis's party came upon Clark as he struggled up the chill Beaverhead, back in the land of present-day Montana.

Sacagawea had been walking with Charbonneau ahead of Clark. Suddenly, she began sucking her fingers and dancing for joy; among these people she had been suckled as a baby. A girl rushed out of a group of Indian women and threw her arms around the Bird Woman; captured by the warring Hidatsas with Sacagawea, she had managed to escape and rejoin her people.

The captains called on Sacagawea to interpret at a council. She sat down near them, only to spring from her place when she saw Cameahwait. It was an instant out of a dream, so incredible, so improbable, that she could utter no words.

Cameahwait was her brother. She ran to him, threw her blanket around him, and wept.

The site of the reunion now lies deep beneath the water of Clark Canyon Reservoir south of Dillon.

I could easily imagine Cameahwait as Lewis saw him, his "ferce eyes and lank jaws grown meager for

"...relinquished all...hope of my favorite boat and ordered her to be sunk in the water, that the skins might become soft in order the better to take her in peices... and deposited the iron fraim....adieu to my boat...."
Journal of Captain Lewis, July 9, 1805, near Great Falls, Montana

the want of food," as he told of the forbidding land ahead. With stick in hand, I re-enacted for the children a scene such as might have happened on that lonely prairie. "See here," I explained, pointing to little piles of dirt that I had heaped up. "Those are mountains. See how close together they are. And here," I said, drawing a line, "is what today we call the Lemhi River. And over there, that's the Salmon.

"But look." I shoved more dirt close to the lines. "See how the mountains crowd the banks. And see how wriggly I've made the lines. Such rough water would be extremely difficult to travel by canoe."

Danny tossed a stone onto one of my mountains. "That's a bear," he said, not caring that Cameahwait had warned the captains there would be

few animals in that country for the men to kill and eat—not even bears.

Cameahwait's information "if true is alarming," wrote Clark. On August 18 he took an advance party of 11 men up the Lemhi Pass and across the Continental Divide to reconnoiter the country for himself, while Lewis stayed behind to cache the canoes, pack baggage, bargain with the Indians, and learn what he could of the mountains ahead.

It was Lewis's 31st birthday. Moodily, he reflected that he had "in all human probability now existed about half the period which I am to remain in this Sublunary world." In that time he felt he had "done but little, very little, indeed, to further the hapiness of the human race, or to advance the information of the succeeding generation." Strange words, I thought, from a man charged with leading the greatest exploratory expedition in his young Nation's history.

On August 21, Clark and his men, together with an old Shoshoni guide they called Toby, reached the junction of the Salmon and the Lemhi, the site of today's city of Salmon, Idaho. They traveled along the Salmon for some 40 miles as it foamed and roared down a rock-strewn channel that would have torn to bits any boats that attempted to sail it. A passage with canoes, Clark concluded, "is entirely impossible." He sent Colter back with a message advising Lewis to obtain as many horses as possible.

With 29 horses and one mule, the entire expedition started northward by land on August 30. Sacagawea and five other Indians, including Toby and three of his sons, accompanied the men.

The explorers trudged along the Lemhi River, often axing their own trail through the thick brush of the Bitterroot Range. Several horses fell, slipping down the steep, craggy hillsides, and soon all the Indian guides except old Toby and one of his sons left.

"...a clear pleasant morning. we Continued on making our canoes as usal. built fires on Some ...to burn them out. found them to burn verry well...."

From the journal of Sergeant Ordway, October 1, 1805, near Orofino, Idaho

Following the North Fork of the Salmon, the expedition re-entered Montana in the vicinity of Lost Trail Pass. August passed into September, bringing foul weather—first snow, then rain and sleet.

It was still summer as my family and I drove through the valley of the Bitterroot River, and I had trouble keeping my eyes on the road, so distracting was the scenery. "The mountains, the forest, the river. What more could anyone want?" Arlette marveled as we passed near the wide valley now known as Ross's Hole. Here on September 4, 1805, the expedition met a party of friendly Indians and purchased 11 more horses. Lewis and Clark called these Indians the Flatheads, although not for some time would they encounter bands of Pacific Coast Indians who practiced reshaping the skulls of their infants.

On September 9, not far from present-day Missoula, Montana, the explorers stopped to rest. In Lolo National Forest nearby we also made camp, and the following morning I hired four strong mountain horses to try the Indian trail old Toby had taken as he led the expedition westward across the Bitterroots into Idaho.

Our "old Toby" was a young ranger named Bill Bradt who led us through the forest over a rarely used rolling, uphill path. The higher we rode, the wider the ridges became. "The expedition traveled in single file through this area, just as we are doing," Bill explained. "Their trail wound around logs and trees and through windblown timber, so the going would have been much slower for Lewis and Clark."

At the tops of some of the higher ridges the timber thickened, the lodgepole pines stood straight and tall, and I pushed the spiny needles of a menacing spruce branch away from my face. Through this same wild country the expedition labored for 11 days. Alternating between a southerly and westerly route, they followed the ridges of the mountains in the footsteps of Nez Percé Indians, who as early as the 1730's had used the trail to get to and from their buffalo hunting grounds to the east.

Through rain and snow and hail the expedition toiled. Desperate, half-starved, the men killed horses for meat, melted snow to drink, and even ate candles. These are "the most terrible mountains I ever beheld," recalled Gass on September 16. A heavy snow fell, and the explorers "could hardly See the old trail," Whitehouse reported.

We dismounted where our route joined the original track of the old Indian path, and while Arlette and the children rested I walked back with Bill to explore. Grass, shrubs, and small trees had invaded the trail, but an unmistakable depression was still evident. Perhaps no place along the entire route of Lewis and Clark had I been more sure of actually walking in their footsteps. Here they had struggled. Here they had suffered.

"I have been wet and as cold in every part as I ever was in my life," wrote Clark; "indeed I was at one time fearfull my feet would freeze in the thin Mockirsons which I wore . . . the party . . . verry cold and much fatigued."

Now back in Idaho, we stopped in a meadow, and Bill tried to quiet our appetites with a staple Indian food. He dug up the bulbs of some camas plants that had gone to seed, and we each took a small bite.

"Tastes like soap," Michele said.

"Tastes like nothing," Danny added.

That night we put some of the raw bulbs in a stew; they sweetened the meal a little, but I wondered how anyone could subsist through the winter —as some Indians apparently did—on such meager fare.

Almost all of the Nez Percé trail is still discernible. In Idaho's Clearwater National Forest a narrow dirt road called the Lolo Trail winds near it, on it, and across it for 100 miles. Driving through this area we found trees mantling the hills and valleys in every direction.

"I think I'd have begun to doubt old Toby," Arlette remarked as we set up our tent with the help of forester Andy Arvish near the same high mountain which Clark and six hunters had crossed on September 18, 1805. It was 800 feet to the top of Sherman Peak, but up we all hiked, over rocks and fallen trees and through thick mountain heather. Some 100 feet from the summit, Danny announced he could go no farther; Arlette stayed behind with him, while the rest of us continued to climb. Reaching the top, 6,658 feet above sea level, we could see, far to the west, "the emence Plain and *leavel* Countrey" that Clark had described.

*T*HE TRIAL OF THE BITTERROOTS was over. Descending to the prairie, Clark came upon a group of Indian lodges, and soon he and his men were dining on buffalo meat, dried salmon, and roots offered by the friendly Nez Percés.

For the third time in only five weeks the expedition had discovered a tribe previously unknown to white men. "Stout likely men, handsom women," Lewis wrote of the Nez Percés as he followed Clark out of the Bitterroots, jubilant at having "tryumphed over the rockey Mountains."

In a forced march of 15 miles Clark had found a navigable stream with pines along its banks that could be cut into canoes. With the chief of the Nez Percés—"a Chearfull man with apparant sincerity" named Twisted Hair—he rode back to the prairie. They found Lewis and the others already assembled, waiting, Lewis wrote, for "the flattering prospect of the final success of the expedition."

About five miles west of today's Orofino, Idaho, they cached their saddles and ammunition. Entrusting their horses to the Nez Percés, they cut down some ponderosa pines and hewed and burned out five canoes to carry them down the swift-flowing Clearwater.

For four days they traveled the river, through numerous bad rapids. By October 9, 1805, old Toby had had enough. He was seen with his son running along the bank, not bothering even to pick up his pay. Perhaps he was "afraid of being cast away passing the rapids," conjectured Gass. Whatever the reason, a great guide was heard from no more.

Reaching the wider Snake, the expedition rode for six days through currents that Whitehouse found "Swifter than any horse could run." They had entered the future state of Washington. Although the Pacific lay not far ahead, they would have to hurry, for the weather was growing colder.

"Some frost this morning and Ice," Clark noted in his journal.

Of the many bird species new to science that Lewis and Clark discovered, these two bear their names: Lewis's woodpecker (Asyndesmus lewis), *upper, and Clark's nutcracker* (Nucifraga columbiana). *The explorers observed both during the summer of 1805.*

MARIE NONNAST BOHLEN

LENGTHS: LEWIS'S
WOODPECKER 10 1/2-11 1/2";
CLARK'S NUTCRACKER 12-13"

FROM CURTIS'S BOTANICAL MAGAZINE, 1863 (ABOVE LEFT); FREDERICK PURSH, FLORA AMERICAE
SEPTENTRIONALIS, 1816 (ABOVE CENTER AND RIGHT); VOLKMAR WENTZEL, NATIONAL GEOGRAPHIC STAFF

INTO THE ROCKY MOUNTAINS

Horses graze a pasture before a backdrop of the Rockies near Three Forks, Montana. No such sight greeted Lewis and Clark, and their anxiety increased as they realized they would soon need horses to cross the mountains. Their route traversed the Bitterroot Range, named for a plant the explorers found there. The bitterroot *(Lewisia rediviva),* opposite at left, also gave its name to a river and became the state flower of Montana. Indians offered some dried fruit of the salmonberry *(Rubus spectabilis),* opposite at center, to Lewis; "it is reather ascid tho' pleasently flavored," he wrote. The captain recorded less enthusiasm for the prairie apple *(Psoralea esculenta),* opposite at right. He found the root, a Plains Indian staple, tasteless and insipid. The explorers described 178 species of plants.

CHARLES M. RUSSELL, 1898, COURTESY THE ROCKWELL GALLERY, CORNING, NEW YORK

TOWARD THE CONTINENTAL DIVIDE

Alert and wary, a party of Piegan Indians hazes a band of stolen horses over moonlit highlands of northern Montana. Undertaking such raids, Plains warriors gained not only horses, symbols of wealth, but also war honors. Far to the southwest, moonglow bathes the slopes of Lemhi Pass (foreground above). Here Lewis and Clark crossed the Continental Divide, then the western boundary of Louisiana Territory.

SHOSHONIS
AT LAST

Greeting Clark (right), Sho-shoni Chief Cameahwait begins to embrace him Indian-fashion. Sacagawea watches intently; moments later as she inter-preted during a council, she recognized the chief as her brother. She had not seen her tribe since the Hidatsas cap-tured her as a child. In previous weeks, as she entered famil-iar country and recognized landmarks, her anticipation had mounted. Her first sight of the Shoshonis brought a joyous reunion (top) with a woman who had been captured with her but later escaped.

J. K. RALSTON, 1964, NATIONAL PARK SERVICE (BELOW); CHARLES M. RUSSELL, 1918, THOMAS GILCREASE INSTITUTE, TULSA

A HOSTILE RIVER IN A WILD LAND

Treacherous Salmon River (opposite) recalls Cameahwait's description as recorded by Lewis: "the perpendicular and even juting rocks so closely hemned in the river that there was no possibil[it]y of passing along the shore; that the bed of the river was obstructed by sharp pointed rocks and the rapidity of the stream such that the whole surface of the river was beat into perfect foam." Known since pioneer days as the "River of No Return," the Salmon today boils untamed through a land that provides a refuge for mountain lions and bighorn sheep (below). A mountain lion the explorers killed not far away measured $7\frac{1}{2}$ feet from nose to tail; they also spotted bighorn sheep among the Bitterroots.

MAURICE G. HORNOCKER (ABOVE)

THE ORDEAL OF THE BITTERROOTS

Following an Indian trail almost obliterated by snow, the expedition climbs the seemingly endless ridges of the Bitterroot Range. "I have been wet and as cold in every part as I ever was in my life," Clark penned on September 16, 1805. Sergeant Gass described the peaks as "the most terrible mountains I ever beheld."

THE WILDERNESS:
TODAY A RARE RESOURCE

September mists soften a bleak landscape of snow-dappled rocks and scarred tree stumps in the Bitterroot Range west of Florence, Montana. A steep granite wall (lower) rises beside One Horse Creek. Much of this wilderness remains virtually unchanged since Lewis and Clark followed Nez Percé Indian trails a few miles to the north. Although the Shoshonis warned of the hardships ahead, the explorers set out with confidence. "I felt perfectly satisfyed, that if the Indians could pass these mountains with their women and Children," wrote Lewis, "that we could also pass them." Six days later, Clark told of the misery they experienced: "The want of provisions together with the dificul[t]y of passing those emence mountains dampened the sperits of the party." After 11 grueling days in the mountains they arrived at a Nez Percé encampment near the navigable Clearwater River. "The pleasure I now felt in having tryumphed over the rockey Mountains and decending once more to a level and fertile country where there was every rational hope of finding a comfortable subsistence for myself and party can be more readily conceived than expressed," exulted Lewis, "nor was the flattering prospect of the final success of the expedition less pleasing."

MISSIONARY ARTIST

Indians of the Rocky Mountains wage bloody intertribal warfare in a
scene from the journals of Father Nicholas Point, S.J., a missionary
among the Flatheads, Coeur d'Alenes, and Blackfeet from 1840
to 1847. Below, a family of Blackfeet heads for a new campsite.

OF THE ROCKIES

Spectators cheer on their favorites at a horse race, a popular sport
among Indians of the northern Rockies. An upended travois becomes
a ladder (below) as Blackfoot women set up camp. A self-taught
artist, Father Point included scores of such scenes in his journals.

PIERCED NOSES AND STOVEPIPE HATS

Shell ornament in the nose of a Nez Percé Indian (above, left) reveals the origin of the tribe's name, meaning "pierced nose" in French. Canadian artist Paul Kane traveled through the territory of today's western Canada and the Northwestern United States between 1845 and 1848. His painting of Caw-wacham, a Chinook woman, and her child shows how the tribe flattened the foreheads of infants. A leather thong passing through holes in a cradleboard pressed a piece of smooth bark against a pad on the baby's forehead. Begun at birth, the process continued for 8 to 12 months. The tribe considered the strange, elongated profile a badge of freedom and did not permit their slaves to take up the practice. In drawings Father Point collected, Indian artists of the northern Rockies recorded interpretations of their own way of life and that of the intruding white man.

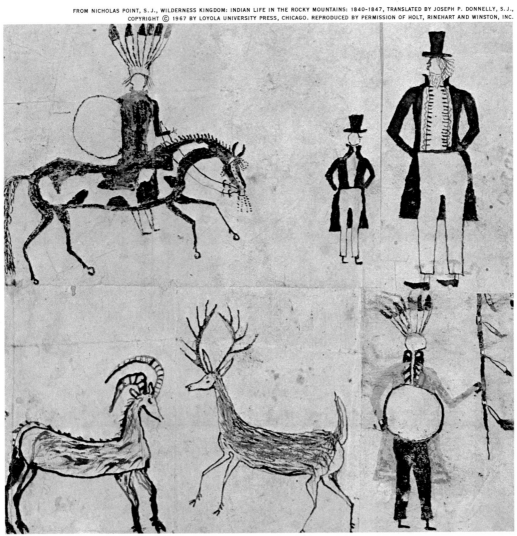

FROM SNOW TO SAND

Golden-yellow flowers of the rabbitbrush *(Chrysothamnus nauseosus)*, right, add a splash of color to the drab, sandy banks of the Columbia River near Wallula, Washington. In the background stands Captains' Rock; it may have inspired Clark to write as he passed, "the countrey rises here about 200 feet above the water and is bordered with black rugid rocks." So few trees grew in the area that the explorers had to buy firewood from local Indians, who also provided food and helped pilot the canoes through treacherous rapids. Today dams tame the Columbia and many of its tributaries. Some 15 miles upstream from the Columbia, the Snake (below) flows silent and serene where the expedition battled white water.

Richard Schlecht

The Ocean in View

CHAPTER SEVEN

WITH MOUNTING HOPES the men steered their boats down the raging torrents of the Columbia—the Great River of the West that would lead them to the sea. The country "rises here about 200 feet above the water and is bordered with black rugid rocks," Clark wrote as the little fleet sped toward a succession of falls and rapids that still barred the way to the Pacific.

Two Nez Percé guides, Twisted Hair and Tetoharsky, who had joined the expedition on the Snake, rode with the explorers. And so did 40 new travelers—dogs purchased for food from the Sokulk Indians upstream.

As Lewis and Clark sailed on, contacts with Indians became more and more frequent. On October 19 they stopped to smoke with four chiefs of the Wallawalla tribe, among them the great Chief Yellept, whom Clark described as "bold handsom...with a dignified countenance about 35 years of age, about 5 feet 8 inches high and well perpotiond."

Such nobility warranted special attention, so the captains presented him with a medal and a handkerchief in addition to the strings of wampum all four chiefs received. But when Yellept asked the white men to delay until midday so his people could come and welcome them, the voyagers graciously excused themselves and hurried onward, promising to stop for a few days on their return.

On what today is the Washington side of the Columbia, Clark spied "a

"...I deturmined to pass through this place notwithstanding the horrid appearance of this agitated gut swelling, boiling & whorling in every direction, which from the top of the rock did not appear as bad as when I was in it...."
From the journal of Captain Clark, October 24, 1805, near The Dalles, Oregon.
Drawing of coho salmon (above) by Clark; Missouri Historical Society.

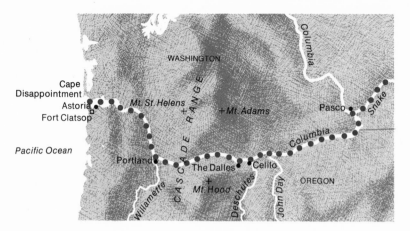

Challenging roaring rapids in their dugout canoes, the men swept down the Columbia. Plagued by rain, hail, and high tides, they searched the north bank unsuccessfully for a site for their winter camp. After crossing the river they built Fort Clatsop. There they spent the winter of 1805-06 and prepared for the return trip.

high mountain of emence hight covered with Snow." He guessed the peak to be Mount St. Helens, which the British sea captain George Vancouver had seen from the mouth of the Columbia 13 years earlier. But Clark was wrong. The peak he saw, now called Mount Adams, loomed far to the east and some 2,600 feet higher than 9,677-foot Mount St. Helens.

Indians often gathered along the river to watch as the explorers passed. Surprised to find no one around as he landed near one group of lodges, Clark went to investigate. He entered a lodge, to find "32 persons men, women and a few children . . . in the greatest agutation, Some crying and ringing there hands, others hanging their heads.

"I gave my hand to them all and made Signs of my friendly dispo[si]-tion," Clark recounted, "and offered the men my pipe to Smok and distributed a fiew Small articles which I had in my pockets." Having placated the Indians in the lodge he moved on to a second, only to find its occupants "more fritened than those of the first."

Eventually Clark learned the cause of the Indians' strange behavior. They had seen a crane shot by Clark fall from the sky and connected the incident with the appearance of clouds overhead. From this they deduced that "we came from the clouds . . . and were not men," Clark wrote. Not until the rest of the expedition arrived and the Indians spotted Sacagawea was their anxiety relieved; "they imediately all came out and appeared to assume new life, the sight of This Indian woman . . . confirmed . . . our friendly intentions, as no woman ever accompanies a war party of Indians in this quarter."

Past swirling rapids and rocks "large and too noumerous to notice," Clark recorded, the expedition headed downriver once more. When the water became too slashing, too boiling to navigate, the men portaged — sometimes hauling their vessels through the swells from along the bank, using ropes made of twisted elk skin.

On the Columbia the explorers soon began to see signs of white men — some of the Indians wore blankets of scarlet and blue cloth. Apparently they had received them in barter from other tribesmen in contact with trading ships along the coast.

And as further proof that the Corps of Discovery was approaching the ocean, the men occasionally noticed Indians who wore seashell ornaments in their pierced noses.

But tumbling, turbulent barriers still stood in the way of the expedition. Suddenly the Columbia split into narrow channels, and just ahead foamed a wild cataract.

Driving toward the modern-day town of Celilo, Oregon, my family and I found neither raging river nor foaming falls. We were more than a decade too late. Water backing up from The Dalles Lock and Dam has inundated the once-awesome Celilo Falls; indeed a whole complex of dams on the Columbia has turned the rushing river that Lewis and Clark knew into a chain of placid pools.

For two days the fearsome cataract slowed the expedition. Baggage had to be portaged and the empty boats carried and floated over the barrier. In the rapids below the falls one of the boats broke loose, but a group of helpful Indians retrieved it.

The Indians along the river had been friendly up to this point, but beyond the falls the captains heard an ugly rumor: Warlike Indians downriver intended to attack the expedition. Constantly on the alert, Lewis and Clark simply rechecked the party's arms and ammunition; to them the real treachery lay not along the bank but on the river.

Ahead roared the Short and Long Narrows—the Dalles of the Columbia—nine miles of wild, rushing water. Reaching the Short Narrows, Clark surveyed the situation: "at this place the water of this great river is compressed into a chanel between two rocks not exceeding *forty five* yards wide and continues for a $\frac{1}{4}$ of a mile when it again widens. . . . The whole of the Current of this great river must at all Stages pass thro' this narrow channel."

*P*ORTAGING the heavy canoes would be too laborious, too time-consuming. The captains turned to Cruzatte, their skilled waterman. He agreed that "by good Stearing we could pass down Safe," wrote Clark, "accordingly I deturmined to pass through this place notwithstanding the horrid appearance of this agitated gut swelling, boiling & whorling in every direction."

Groups of curious Indians gathered on the rocks above the river to watch. To their astonishment all five of the canoes safely breasted the hazardous rapids—though not entirely without incident; "one of the canoes nearly fi[lled] running through the rapids waves & whorl pools," Whitehouse reported.

Below the Long Narrows the explorers paused to caulk their battered canoes and to bid goodbye to Twisted Hair and Tetoharsky. The chiefs had agreed to stay with Lewis and Clark through the rapids, but now it was time for them to return home.

On October 28 the expedition set sail again, and over the next few days the explorers saw more signs that the coast was not far ahead. In villages they found more scarlet and blue cloth, brass tea kettles, a British musket, a cutlass, a sword, and even Indians dressed in round hats and sailor jackets.

About 45 miles below the Dalles, the river surged through a deep gorge. For seven tortuous miles the voyagers shouldered their equipment and supplies, floating their unloaded canoes through the roiling water of the series of cascades that one day would give their name to the Cascade Range through which they flow.

Finally, on October 31, beyond the worst of the rapids, the river began to widen. To Clark the water "had everry appearance of being effected by the tide." The rise and fall of the tide became unmistakable in the dark, cloudy days that followed. On November 4 Ordway wrote, "the tide Ebbs and flowes abt 3 feet at this place."

On the fifth it rained the greater part of the day; "we are all wet cold and disagreeable," Clark recounted. Again on the sixth: "Cloudy with rain all day.... had large fires made ... and dried our bedding." Rocky cliffs rose on either side, and the explorers had trouble finding a place to camp beyond reach of the tide.

November 7 began no better—"the fog so thick we could not See across the river," Clark noted. But then the fog cleared, and at last the elated captain could write *"Ocian in view! O! the joy."*

Clark well may have mistaken the large expanse of the river's mouth for the ocean itself; today it is not possible to see the Pacific from this point, just east of Astoria, Oregon. But hearing the sound of waves breaking, he was satisfied the Corps of Discovery had reached the great Pacific, "which we been so long anxious to See."

The hazards of their journey were still not over. Time and again high tides and crashing waves forced the explorers to stop to seek refuge on narrow, rocky banks.

Great pieces of driftwood—trees nearly 200 feet long and as much as 7 feet thick—threatened to crush the canoes. In pounding rain the men unloaded their canoes and raised their baggage on logs out of reach of the roaring, storm-driven swells. The men were "as wet as water could make them," Clark wrote, but they remained "chearfull and anxious to See further into the Ocian."

A heavy rain—not unlike that which Lewis and Clark had faced—beat against the windshield of our car as we drove across Astoria Bridge over the Columbia from Oregon into Washington. A few miles north, near the town of McGowan, I stopped to walk alone to the water's edge. Unmindful of the rain, I stood and watched as the tide washed in, spilling bits of driftwood onto the rocky shore.

Somewhere near this spot Lewis and Clark first had seen the breakers of the Pacific. From their camp not far away, Clark had "directed all the men who wished to see more of the main *Ocian* to prepare themselves to Set out with me."

Where he and his party of 11 had trekked on November 18, 1805, we now drove—through the community of Illwaco to Cape Disappointment, named by a British sea captain in 1788 after a vain search for the mouth of the Columbia.

From atop this thick, tree-covered arm of land rising in places to about

150 feet above the shoreline, Clark's group had looked out onto the Pacific. There they had beheld "with estonishment the high waves dashing against the rocks & this emence Ocian."

Clark and his men returned to camp in time to watch Lewis bargain with some Chinook Indians for a robe made of two sea otter skins—"the finest fur I ever saw," Sergeant Gass declared. Almost desperate to have it, the captains offered blankets, red and white beads, a handkerchief, a silver dollar, and even Clark's watch. The Indians would settle for nothing other than blue beads, but the explorers had no more.

Sacagawea saved the day. She gave the captains her belt of blue beads, and the much desired robe was theirs. In exchange for the belt, Clark gave Sacagawea a "coate of Blue Cloth."

Rain continued to pelt us as we left the cape, recalling the long siege of rough weather the expedition had encountered. "O! how horriable is the day," Clark wrote on November 22, "waves brakeing with great violence against the Shore throwing the Water into our Camp &c. all wet and confind to our Shelters." And six days later: "O! how disagreeable is our Situation dureing this dreadfull weather."

Between the dates of these dour observations, Lewis and Clark put the question of a permanent location for their winter camp to a vote. Hunting had been bad on the north side of the river. Should they proceed to the south? The vote was almost unanimous that they should.

Even Sacagawea had a vote. "Janey," as Clark began calling her, spoke "in favor of a place where there is plenty of Pota[toe]s," her mind on the growing hunger of the men, whose daily diet of pounded fish mixed

"Great joy . . . we are in view of the Ocian . . . which we been so long anxious to See. and the roreing or noise made by the waves brakeing on the rockey Shores (as I suppose) may be heard disti[n]ctly. . . ."

From the journal of Captain Clark, November 7, 1805, near Astoria, Oregon

with salt water was making many of them ill. Sacagawea turned to Clark. She had made a little piece of bread from some flour "which She had reserved for her child." It had become wet and a bit sour, but wouldn't the captain like to have it?

With "great satisfaction," Clark ate the bread, "it being the only mouthfull I had tasted for Several months past."

The explorers crossed to the south side of the Columbia, and on November 29 Lewis took five men and set out "in surch of an eligible place for our winters residence." When, after five days, they had not returned, Clark grew anxious; "no account of Capt. Lewis," he wrote. "I fear Some accident has taken place in his craft or party."

Clark's fears proved groundless, for the next day Lewis and his men returned—and with good news: They had found a suitable place for the expedition's winter quarters about three miles away. On December 7

"... the swells continued high all the evening & we are compelled to form an Encampment on a Point scercely room sufficent for us all to lie cleare of the tide water.... we are all wet and disagreeable, as we have been ... for several days...."

Journal of Captain Clark, November 8, 1805, near the mouth of the Columbia

the entire party moved to the site, located in a stand of lofty pine trees along a river about seven miles inland from the "Great Western Ocian" —"I cant say Pasific," Clark joked wryly, "as since I have seen it, it has been the reverse."

Life would not soon change for the better. In the days that followed, Pryor dislocated his shoulder, Werner strained his knee, and insects got under the men's clothes and into their bedding. "The flees were so troublesome last night," Clark wrote on December 12, "that I made but a broken nights rest."

Gradually Fort Clatsop took form, built of the "streightest & most butifullest logs" the men could find and named for a tribe of friendly Indians who lived nearby.

Clark's plan, as sketched on the inside cover of his field book, called for a stockade 50 feet square, with two rows of common-walled cabins

Richard Schlecht

fronting on two sides of a 20-foot-wide parade ground. The ends of the parade ground not bounded by rows of cabins were to be enclosed with sturdy log walls and gates.

By December 14 the men had completed the log work on their cabins, and the captains set them to "finishing a house to put meat into," Clark wrote, noting that "all our last Supply of Elk has Spoiled in the repeeted rains." Snow and hail soon followed, making the weather all the more disagreeable and temporarily holding up work. But by the 20th, four of the cabins had been roofed, and three days later Lewis and Clark moved into their still-unfinished hut.

*F*OUR AND A HALF MILES southwest of Astoria stands a reproduction of Fort Clatsop, built on the site of the original. To pay a visit was, of course, a must.

"Come prepared for an authentic winter," the fort's superintendent, James M. Thomson, had cautioned us. "During the captains' four-month stay here only 12 days were without rain, and the winter we've been having is a good sample." When we arrived on New Year's Day, fully prepared in our rain gear, it did indeed rain. But fortunately we found none of the "ticks, flies and other insects" that tormented Sergeant Gass that first day of 1806.

One hundred sixty-three years later to the day we could boast of being the first visitors of the year to the Fort Clatsop National Memorial, administered by the National Park Service. Mr. Thomson escorted us through the main gates of the stockade. He told us three Finnish carpenters, experts at building log cabins, had reconstructed the fort in 1955.

"Nothing was found of the original fort—it just gradually crumbled away," Mr. Thomson explained. "But the reproduction faithfully follows the original, built to look like the fort must have looked on the day after the explorers left to return home."

Just inside and to the right of the gate we took refuge in a room which turned out to be the Charbonneau family quarters. Before I could ask a question, Michele wanted to know where Jean Baptiste slept.

"There was just that one bed," Mr. Thomson told us, pointing to a bare cedar frame near the wall. "No crib for the baby. Baptiste would have slept with his parents."

Inspecting the sparse furnishings in the room, I wondered why only one chair stood at the table. "Only one adult ate at a time," Mr. Thomson explained. "Sacagawea would have served Charbonneau, and then she would have eaten with the baby."

In the best-furnished room, the captains' quarters next door, we found two beds and two "belly-boards," stand-up writing desks, at either end of the room, and before a huge fireplace a table and two chairs. As we talked Mr. Thomson lit a fire to help ward off the dampness.

Next we entered the orderly room, where the sergeants would have slept, and then we stepped into the meat house, the last room in the row, where deer and elk would have been cured over a firepit.

Rarely was the meat house filled that year, for game proved hard to find. On Christmas Day of 1805 the explorers dined on unsalted, spoiled elk meat, spoiled pounded fish, and a few roots—"a bad Christmass diner"—Clark wrote.

But the men were "Snugly fixed in their huts" and those who used tobacco shared in the supply the captains distributed; the others received presents of silk handkerchiefs.

Ordway lamented that the party had no whiskey. But he could not complain, for the men were in good health, "which we esteem more than all the ardent Spirits in the world."

On the morning of January 1, 1806, Lewis awoke to the sound of a volley of small arms fired by the men "in front of our quarters to usher in the new year . . . the only mark of rispect which we had it in our power to pay this celebrated day."

Though they ate better than they had at Christmas, their real repast, as Lewis put it, "consisted principally in the anticipation of the 1st day of January 1807, when in the bosom of our friends we hope to participate in the mirth and hilarity of the day, and when with the zest given by the recollection of the present, we shall completely, both mentally and corporally, enjoy the repast which the hand of civilization has prepared for us."

Passing the sentry house outside the orderly room, we followed the children as they dashed across the parade grounds to explore the three squad rooms where the enlisted men lived. We left the fort through the rear gate and paused at a woodpile—"probably like one the expedition had"—Mr. Thomson told us. To our right nearby, between two high spruce trees, we found a rack for hanging game and beneath it a butchering table.

Deer and elk still roam the 125 acres of the memorial site, tracking through evergreens and drinking from springs. From behind the fort a trail leads to one of the springs, perhaps the very one that produced the expedition's main water supply.

Another trail in front of the fort closely followed a path used by Bratton, Gibson, Willard, Joseph Field, and Pvt. Peter Wiser as they hiked to the ocean on December 28 to make salt.

For more than a week the captains did not hear from the men, and fears grew that something had happened to the group. But then Willard and Wiser returned, bringing with them "a specemine of the salt of about a gallon," which Lewis found "excellent, fine, strong, & white . . . a great treat to myself and most of the party."

About 10 miles southwest of the fort, on Lewis and Clark Way—a serene beachfront street in the resort city of Seaside—we inspected a distilling stove like the one the explorers used. Five metal kettles stood on the stones used for the fireplace; here the men went through the laborious process of boiling sea water to extract salt. In seven weeks they obtained a total of 20 gallons of salt, carefully storing most of it in kegs for use in curing meat during the return journey.

In addition to their gallon of salt, Willard and Wiser brought back some

blubber from a whale that Indians had found stranded on the beach. Lewis ordered part of the fat cooked, "and found it very pallitable and tender." Clark determined to set out the following morning to attempt to purchase "a parcel of the blubber" to add some luster to their dull diet.

Learning of Clark's plans, Sacagawea implored the captains to let her go along. "She observed that She had traveled a long way with us to See the great waters," Clark recorded, "and that now that monstrous fish was also to be Seen, She thought it verry hard that She could not be permitted to See either (She had never yet been to the Ocian)."

On January 6 Clark and a party of 12, plus Sacagawea and her husband, headed for the shores of the Pacific. After visiting the salt makers they hired an Indian guide to help them reach the whale.

To get there they had to ascend an "emence mountain the top of which was obscured in the clouds." It took two hours to attain the summit of the rocky prominence known today as Tillamook Head. Another peak, to-day's Cape Falcon, still lay ahead. Climbing it the following day, Clark observed "the grandest and most pleasing prospects which my eyes ever surveyed, in my frount a boundless Ocean; to the N. and N.E. the coast as . . . far as my sight could be extended, the Seas rageing with emence wave[s] and brakeing with great force from the rocks of Cape Disa-pointment as far as I could see to the N.W."

"17th. rained all night. air somewhat colder this morning. . . . 18th. frequent showers through the day 19th. frequent and sudden changes during the day wind not so hard as usual. 20th rained all day without intermission. 21st rained all night. . . . 22nd. rain continued . . . greater part of the night."

From meteorological data kept by Captain Lewis,
March 1806, Fort Clatsop, Oregon

When Clark and his party finally reached the whale they found that the Indians had stripped the monstrous mammal down to its skeleton. Reluctantly, the Indians sold the white men about 300 pounds of blubber and a few gallons of oil.

"Small as this stock is," wrote Clark, "I prise it highly; and thank providence for directing the whale to us; and think him much more kind to us than he was to jonah, having Sent this Monster to be *Swallowed by us* in Sted of *Swallowing of us* as jonah's did."

With nothing more monstrous on our minds than starfish and sea anemones, my family and I strolled along the same wide stretch of splendid coast where Clark had found the skeleton of the whale, and watched as the waves boiled onto the beach.

While Michele washed sand from some shells she had found and Danny poked a stick at a troublesome crab, Arlette and I splashed up to our boot tops in the heaving surf.

The sounds of gulls crying overhead and waves crashing against the shore suddenly made us realize we too had explored half a continent. And, like Lewis and Clark, we had achieved our goal.

In dreary rain and dismal fog the winter wore on. The captains worked at their journals, and the men whiled away the time trading with Indians, repairing weapons, dressing skins, and making clothes for their homeward journey. Although game was hardly abundant, everyone seemed contented with his fare.

And thanks in no small part to Drouillard's good aim, no one went hungry. On one occasion he killed seven elk in a single day, causing Lewis to comment, "I scarcely know how we should subsist were it not for the exertions of this excellent hunter."

To the captains "a marrowbone a piece and a brisket of boiled Elk that had the appearance of a little fat on it" made a supper of "high stile," in Lewis's words—"in fact fiesting," Clark agreed.

Often during the long months the men turned to thoughts of home, but it would have been foolish to try to start back much before the first of April. From the Indians Lewis and Clark learned that in winter snow lay knee-deep along the plains of the Columbia and to depths of 20 feet in the Rockies. The mountains would not be passable until June.

"Why didn't President Jefferson send a ship to bring them home?" Arlette asked. She posed a question that has puzzled historians for decades. The best guess is that Jefferson did not want to run the risk of offending Spain by venturing too near its many settlements farther down the Pacific Coast.

UT THE PRESIDENT had recognized that the explorers might "find it imprudent to hazard a return" by land and instead seek to obtain passage aboard a trading vessel; he had provided his former secretary with a "letter of general credit" for just such a circumstance.

The letter authorized the captain "to draw on the Secretaries of State, of the Treasury, of War & of the Navy of the U. S. according as you may find your draughts will be most negociable, for the purpose of obtaining money or necessaries for yourself & your men."

Lewis never got a chance to use the document, but unknown to him at the time there was a ship in the vicinity—and an American ship at that.

The brig *Lydia,* commanded by Capt. Samuel Hill, had left Boston in August 1804 bound for China by way of Cape Horn and the northwest Pacific Coast. For several weeks in November 1805 the *Lydia* had plied the waters in and near the mouth of the Columbia, trading with the Indians for furs. But though Lewis and Clark learned of at least a dozen ships that had visited the coast earlier, no mention of the *Lydia*'s activity ever reached the expedition.

January passed into February, and February into March, with little letup in the dreary weather. It rained as usual on March 23, a Sunday, but about noon the weather improved, and the men loaded their canoes.

On that day of their departure Clark recorded: "at this place we had wintered and remained from the 7th of Decr. 1805 to this day and have lived as well as we had any right to expect, and we can say that we were never one day without 3 meals of some kind a day either pore Elk meat or roots, notwithstanding the repeated fall of rain."

And so they began the long journey home.

First map of the Columbia River, made by Clark, relied on information from Chief Yellept of the Wallawallas. Clark presented him with a peace medal, similar to the one at right. Coastal Indians often reciprocated with gifts of necklaces made with Dentalium shells, their most prized trade goods.

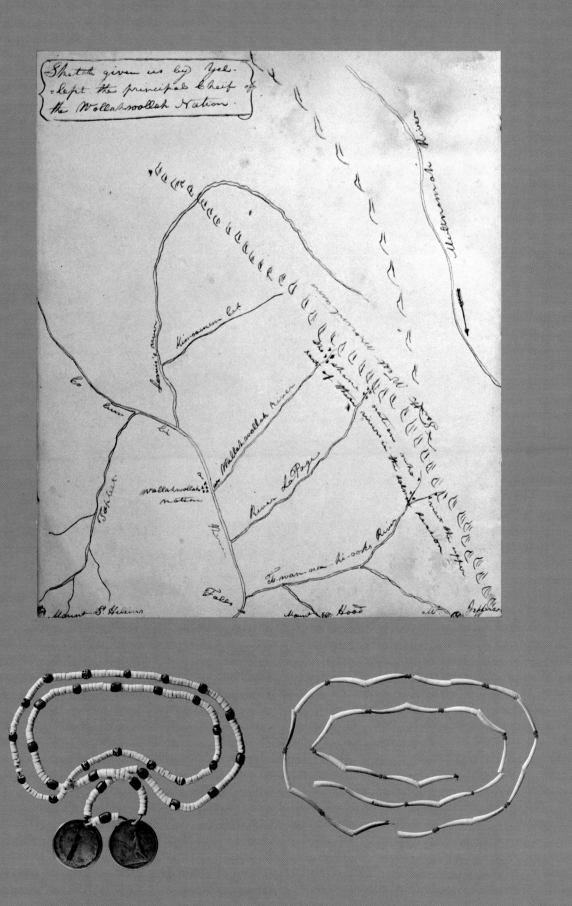

DESCENDING THE COLUMBIA TO THE PACIFIC

Morning mist drops a veil across the Columbia River near Washington's Beacon Rock State Park. As their canoes carried them toward the Pacific, the explorers found a lush land "as grateful to the eye as it is useful in supplying us with fuel."

INDIANS OF THE COLUMBIA
FISH A BOUNTIFUL RIVER

At Kettle Falls on the Columbia River, Colville Indians gig, club, and trap salmon leaping upstream to spawn in a painting by Paul Kane. A Colville village that he visited (right) had lodges "formed of mats of rushes stretched on poles. A flooring is made of sticks, raised three or four feet from the ground, leaving the space beneath it entirely open, and forming a cool, airy, and shady place, in which to hang their salmon to dry." Near here, Sergeant Ordway recorded salmon "jumping very thick," and Clark saw an estimated 10,000 pounds of dried salmon in baskets. Not knowing of the fish's spawning cycle, he wondered at the profusion: "The number of dead Salmon on the Shores & floating in the river is incredible."

DEATHLESS WESTERN GRANDEUR

Finespun Latourell Falls (above), 249 feet high, pitches from the steep sides of a gorge gouged by the Columbia. "Down these heights frequently descend the most beautiful cascades," wrote the explorers. At right a stream threads Oneonta Gorge in Oregon. Lichens, ferns, and golden mimulus blanket its precipitous walls. Inclement weather obscured much of the scenery for the voyagers; "the fog So thick...that we cannot See more than one hundred yards distance," said Private Whitehouse on November 3, 1805.

AN EXPLODING PEAK,

Mt. St. Helens in Washington spews a fiery bouquet; Indians watch in wonder and awe. They thought that the volcano housed a race of cannibals and refused to accompany artist Paul Kane on a closer visit, even when offered bribes. An eruption three years earlier, painted by Kane from the Indians' descriptions, "threw up burning

A VANISHING CULTURE

stones and lava to an immense height, which ran in burning torrents down its snow-clad sides." A bird carved in rock (left), found near The Dalles Dam, spreads feathered wings. Today dams have inundated most Indian artifacts of the region. Chief Man-ce-muckt of the Nez Percés posed for Kane wearing a fur hat and fox-skin cape.

AMERICANS AT THE MOUTH
OF THE COLUMBIA

Stars and Stripes flies from the masts of *Columbia Rediviva,* commanded by Capt. Robert Gray of Boston,
who discovered and named the Columbia River in May
1792. "Seamen and tradesmen employed in their various departments," the Captain logged, as the men
scrubbed the sides of the ship and ferried supplies and
fresh water from shore. Lewis and Clark hoped to find
such a ship when they reached the coast; Jefferson had
instructed them to send "two of your trusty people back
by sea . . . with a copy of your notes. and should you be
of opinion that the return of your party by the way they
went will be eminently dangerous, then ship the whole,
& return by sea by way of Cape Horn or the Cape of
good Hope as you shall be able." The brig *Lydia* out of
Boston sailed nearby waters in 1805-06, but both parties
remained ignorant of the other's presence. At right
the explorers confront a group of Chinook Indians
near the mouth of the Columbia in November 1805.
Sacagawea, standing near Lewis, addresses them in sign
language. Artist Charles M. Russell made the familiar
mistake of over-emphasizing her role: During most of
the journey she remained quietly in the background.

HEWITT JACKSON, 1965, OREGON HISTORICAL SOCIETY; AMON CARTER MUSEUM, FORT WORTH (BELOW LEFT)

THE SECOND WINTER — ON THE COAST

Sitka spruces tower above Fort Clatsop, a reproduction of the one the explorers built near the ocean. Construction began on December 8, 1805, and by Christmas everyone had moved in. The long winter passed slowly, with cold rains practically every day and little to eat except fish and "pore Elk." Between December 1 and March 20 the hunters killed 131 of the animals. Cruzatte's fiddle, probably similar to the one above, helped while away the time. Friendly Clatsop Indians visited frequently and received the fort as a gift when the explorers departed in the spring. Below, summer verdure frames a dugout like the ones used by the Corps of Discovery.

ON THE CONTINENT'S WESTERN EDGE:
A MISTY VISION

"...the grandest and most pleasing prospects which my eyes ever surveyed," wrote Clark on January 8, 1806; "in my frount a boundless Ocean...the coast as...far as my sight could be extended, the Seas rageing with emence wave[s] brakeing with great force." Beneath gray skies, surf still pummels boulders off the Oregon coast; Haystack Rock, a familiar landmark, lies offshore (center above). As the explorers' thoughts turned homeward, Lewis penned, "the leafing of the hucklebury riminds us of Spring." On March 23 they started back.

Going Home at Last

CHAPTER EIGHT

BY THE SPRING OF 1806 most Americans had given the expedition up for lost. Thomas Jefferson was among the few who still held out hope, and he had but scant information on which to base his confidence. Not since the keelboat's return to St. Louis had he received any word from his former secretary. He knew that Lewis and Clark had left Fort Mandan for the wilderness to the west, but a year had passed since then.

From various sources came rumors that the explorers had been shot, or tomahawked, or drowned, or killed by wild animals. One story even had them laboring as slaves of Spaniards in Mexican mines.

Laboring they were, but in high spirits, up the Columbia.

As I prepared to retrace their homeward path, I spread out a map to compare the expedition's westward and eastward routes. Michele was quick to notice how closely the lines ran together, then how suddenly one swung away from the other.

Much of the return journey would cover familiar ground — the trail the explorers had followed westward to the Pacific. But there also would be new routes to conquer, I explained, and more information to gather for President Jefferson.

With the aid of 10 horses obtained in costly bartering with Indians along the river, the expedition completed the difficult portage of the falls of the Columbia.

"...J. Fields ... turned about to look for his gun and saw the fellow just runing off with her ... he called to his brother who instantly jumped up and pursued ... him and R. Fields as he seized his gun stabed the indian to the heart....."

From the journal of Captain Lewis, July 27, 1806, in northwestern Montana. Captain Clark sketched Indian canoes (above) seen on a tributary of the Columbia; Missouri Historical Society.

On April 27 the voyagers once again reached the land of the Wallawallas. Chief Yellept, whom Lewis reported "much gratifyed at seeing us return," had some advice for the captains: By following an old Indian trail that bypassed the Snake River they would be able to save at least 80 miles. A week later the explorers were in Nez Percé country, where they had left their horses for safekeeping the previous fall. But there they would have to delay, for the spurs of the Bitterroots lay deep in snow; "that icy barier" separated the expedition "from all which makes life esteemable," Lewis wrote.

Where the town of Kamiah, Idaho, now rises from the fertile bank of the South Fork of the Clearwater River, Lewis and Clark and their men camped and whiled away whole weeks, seeking food, taking inventory of dwindling trade goods, running foot races with the Indians, and treating them for various ailments.

Clark's prowess as a wilderness doctor brought him 40 or 50 patients a day. During the journey he had acquired quite a reputation as a medicine man, giving out laxatives, liniments, and eyewash, cleaning and dressing sores and wounds, and draining abscesses.

Such efforts had "given those nativs an exolted oppinion of my skill as a phi[si]cian," he recalled.

A number of the explorers themselves complained of illness: Frazer, Joseph Field, and Wiser of headaches, and York and Howard of colic. But in worst condition was Bratton; he suffered from a lumbar ailment that had incapacitated him all the way from Fort Clatsop.

Shields proposed a remedy. With the captains' approval he dug a hole 3 feet across and 4 feet deep, lined it with rocks, and kindled a fire to heat the stones. Once the rocks were heated, Bratton let himself be lowered naked to a seat rigged in the hole.

The men arched willow poles over him, covering them with blankets to hold in the heat, and Bratton poured water onto the stones. Clouds of steam billowed around him.

After 20 minutes of this treatment Bratton was taken out and "suddonly plunged in cold water twise and was then immediately returned to the sweat hole," Lewis wrote. There the private stayed for 45 minutes more, drinking copious amounts of mint tea. Finally he was "taken out covered up in several blankets and suffered to cool gradually."

The experiment soon proved its worth. The next day Bratton was walking about, nearly free of pain, well on his way to recovery.

The treatment had worked so well that Lewis and Clark decided to try it on a Nez Percé chief who had been unable to move his arms and legs for three years. The men lowered him into the hole, duplicating the routine that had been so beneficial to Bratton.

Again the "medicine" did its work. After three treatments the invalid chief could move his legs and wiggle his toes and use his arms and hands; "he washed his face himself today," Lewis reported on May 29, "which he has been unable to do."

On June 15, as the Clearwater rose high from melting snow, the

expedition struck out in full strength into the Bitterroots. All but two of the horses Lewis and Clark had left with the Nez Percés had been recovered. These, together with the ones that they had obtained earlier, added up to more than 60, enough to carry the expedition over the mountains.

The men had traveled some 50 tortuous miles when the indispensable woodsman Drouillard informed the captains that there was no hope of obtaining sufficient food for the horses. Snow still lay too deep, up to 15 feet in places.

Lewis pondered the problem: "if we proceeded and should get bewildered in these mountains the certainty was that we should loose all our horses and consequently our baggage inst[r]uments perhaps our papers." Storing their baggage and food on scaffolds, the men turned back, "the first time...on this long tour that we have ever been compelled to retreat," Lewis lamented.

A week later they were back on the trail, this time with three Indians as guides — obtained at the cost of two rifles. Retrieving their supplies, they recrossed Sherman Peak and began the long march into modern-day Montana. By June 29 they were bidding "adew to the Snow," as a happy Clark put it, and soon they were soaking in hot water that poured from the base of a cliff at today's Lolo Hot Springs.

At Traveller's Rest, near present-day Missoula, Montana, the expedition paused. Here Lewis and Clark had planned to divide the party. Lewis with nine men — Drouillard, Gass, Thompson, McNeal, Werner, Frazer, the Field brothers, and Silas Goodrich — would ride east to the Great Falls of the Missouri. From there they would swing northward to explore the Marias as a possible route into the fur country of Canada, then return to the Missouri and rejoin Clark at its confluence with the Yellowstone.

Clark would take the rest of the expedition over the 1805 route, pick up the canoes which had been cached on the way west, and sail downstream

"...we gave the sick Cheif a severe sweat today, shortly after which he could move one of his legs and thyes and work his toes pretty well, the other leg he can move a little; his fingers and arms seem to be almost entirely restored."

From the journal of Captain Lewis, May 30, 1806, near Kamiah, Idaho

to the Three Forks. There Clark's party also would split up. Ordway with nine men would travel down the Missouri, pick up the supplies left at the Great Falls, and meet Lewis at the Marias, while Clark would head east to explore the Yellowstone.

On July 3, 1806, the captains went their separate ways. "All arrangements being now compleated for carrying into effect the several scheemes we had planed for execution on our return, we saddled our horses and set out," wrote Lewis. "I took leave of my worthy friend and companion Capt. Clark and the party that accompanyed him. I could not avoid feeling much concern on this occasion although I hoped this seperation was only momentary."

The Indian guides set out with Lewis and his party, but they soon turned back, afraid of running into their enemies, the Hidatsas. The men turned eastward, and on July 7 they crossed the Continental Divide over Lewis and Clark Pass. Six days later they reached the Great Falls.

The trip went virtually without incident, except for one encounter with a bear. A grizzly caused McNeal's horse to bolt and throw its rider. McNeal leaped to his feet, whacked the bear over the head with his rifle, and clambered up a nearby willow tree. There he remained for three hours until the bear gave up and wandered off. As Lewis recounted the incident, it seemed to him that fate had treated the expedition kindly as far as grizzlies were concerned, "or some of us would long since have fallen a sacrifice to their farosity."

Leaving Gass and five others to wait for Ordway and help him portage

"...I was in the act of firing on the Elk ... when a ball struck my left thye about an inch below my hip joint ...I instantly supposed that Cruzatte had shot me in mistake for an Elk as I was dressed in brown leather and he cannot see very well...."

From the journal of Captain Lewis, August 11, 1806, near Williston, North Dakota

the falls, Lewis, Drouillard, and the Field brothers rode off to explore the Marias. The captain had hoped to "avoid an interview" with the fierce Hidatsas or Blackfeet who roamed the area north of the Missouri, but on July 26 he spied "a very unpleasant sight"—eight Indians traveling with about 30 horses. As he had done so many times before, Lewis acted boldly, ordering his men forward to meet the band.

Dismounting, the white men smoked with the Indians and learned they were Piegans of the Blackfoot confederacy. As they camped together that night, the suspicious Lewis kept the first watch, then turned the lookout over to Reuben Field.

Shortly after daybreak, a loud cry roused the captain from his slumber: "damn you let go my gun."

It was Drouillard, scuffling with a Piegan.

In the struggle that followed, Reuben stabbed another Indian through the heart, and Lewis shot a third he caught trying to drive off the explorers' horses. As the warrior fell to his knees, he returned the captain's fire, narrowly missing Lewis's head.

The rest of the party fled, but as a result of the melee two Piegans lay dead, the only Indians killed on the entire journey.

Fearing reprisal, the explorers rode swiftly to the junction of the Marias and Missouri. Reaching the confluence the next day they sighted, to their "unspeakable satisfaction," six dugouts speeding downstream. Reunited, Lewis's men and Ordway's group started down the Missouri, "extreemly anxious to reach the entrance of the Yellowstone river where we expect to join Capt. Clark and party."

Clark was doing his best. With 20 men, Sacagawea and her son, and 50 horses, he had reached the Three Forks after crossing the Continental Divide via Gibbons Pass and setting off down the Jefferson in canoes reclaimed from their cache of the year before. From the Three Forks, Ordway had taken his group down the Missouri, while Clark and his party struck out overland.

On horseback they followed a fork of the Gallatin toward Bozeman Pass. At last, about 10 miles beyond the pass—near the present city of Livingston, Montana—they reached the Roche Jaune, or Yellowstone, named by Frenchmen many years before for the grayish-yellow rocks that ribbed the hills along its banks.

For four days Clark and his party followed the course of the rushing Yellowstone on horseback. Finally, near Columbus, Montana, they found trees large enough for dugouts. No sooner had they completed work on their boats than a band of Crow Indians stole 24 of their 50 horses. On July 24 Pryor, Shannon, Windsor, and Hall left to drive the remaining animals overland, and the rest of the party continued downstream.

The following day Clark came upon a huge sandstone formation rising 200 feet above the flat plain. Stopping to investigate, the captain named the stone bulwark "Pompys Tower" after Sacagawea's son, using the nickname he had given him. Pompeys Pillar it is called today—this bold landmark that stands 28 miles east of Billings, Montana.

With Mrs. Don C. Foote, who owns the bulwark and some 200 acres of land surrounding it, my family and I went to inspect the pillar. We climbed up its eastern face along the same route Clark had taken as he sought to survey the surrounding valley. Past hundreds of names carved over the years we hiked. Finally we reached the most famous autograph of them all—that of Clark himself, still legible and protected from weather and vandals by bronze-framed shatterproof glass. "It's probably the most famous autograph in the West," Mrs. Foote told us proudly.

Nine days after passing Pompeys Pillar, Clark reached the junction of the Yellowstone and the Missouri and set up camp at the same point where the expedition had halted on April 26, 1805. The morning of August 8 he spied, to his surprise, Pryor, Shannon, Hall, and Windsor coming down the Yellowstone in two buffalo-skin bullboats. A band of Crows, Pryor explained, had driven off their horses.

Clark and his reunited group started down the Missouri the following day, figuring that Lewis and his men soon would overtake them. Two days later they encountered "two men from the illinoies"—the first white men they had seen in more than two years—venturing upstream to trap on the Yellowstone.

On August 12 Lewis's boats "hove in Sight," but Clark's joy soon turned to fright, for he found Lewis lying in the white pirogue, a bullet hole in his thigh. While hunting the previous day, Cruzatte—blind in one eye and nearsighted in the other—had mistaken Lewis in his brown leather apparel for an elk.

Clark treated the wound, and the party paddled on. Two days later they were back among the Mandans and Hidatsas, imploring the chiefs to return with them to visit the "Great Father" Jefferson.

Some of the chiefs were fearful of trying to pass through Sioux country, but with the aid of René Jusseaume the captains persuaded the Mandan Chief Big White to make the journey. As a reward for his help, Jusseaume was to go along as official interpreter. He could take his wife and two children, and Big White could take one of his wives and her child for their first look at civilization.

Closer to home than he had been in nearly a year and a half, one member of the expedition—John Colter—chose to turn his back on civilization. He did not want to go home; he would be "lonely" in St. Louis. The two fur trappers bound for the Yellowstone had offered him a share in their venture, and he asked the captains to let him go back west.

The captains agreed and, in Ordway's words, "Settled with him and fitted him out with powder lead and a great number of articles which compleated him for a trapping voiage of two years."

It was time too for Charbonneau, Sacagawea, and little Pompy to leave the expedition, for this land of the Mandans was their home. Charbonneau was discharged and paid $500.33⅓.

Although Sacagawea received nothing, Clark offered to take Pompy to St. Louis and educate him. Charbonneau decided the time was not right. In a year perhaps "the boy would be sufficiently old to leave his mother," Clark wrote, "& he would then take him to me if I would be so freindly as to raise the child for him."

The expedition swept onward, moving farther and farther downstream, closer and closer to home. They stopped at various points—to call at Fort Mandan, and to visit an Arikara village—but not for long. On September 3 the explorers met two boats pushing upstream and learned of news from home: Aaron Burr had killed Alexander Hamilton in a duel two years before; Gen. James Wilkinson had been made Governor of the Louisiana Territory; and "Two British Ships of the line had fired on an American Ship in the port of New York."

The captains stopped briefly to visit the grave of Sergeant Floyd, and two days later they encountered a trader who sold them a whole gallon of whiskey, their "first spiritious licquor...since the 4 of July 1805," Clark recollected.

On September 8 Lewis and Clark reached the site of their first Indian council, having traveled 78 miles; the next day they passed the mouth of the Platte River. September 15 found them at the mouth of the Kansas, and on September 19 they camped for the night at the confluence of the Osage and the Missouri. The following day the men cheered loudly to see cows grazing along the riverbank. They soon would be home.

Nearing La Charrette later the same day, they "Sprung upon their ores." The explorers fired a salute, and five trading boats berthed off the town boomed a reply; "every person, both French and americans," Clark recounted, "seem to express great pleasure at our return, and acknowledged themselves much astonished in seeing us return. They informed us that we were supposed to have been long lost since, and were entirely given out by every person."

EACHING ST. CHARLES the next day, the men saw women walking along the river—the first white women they had seen in two years and four months. With "great dexterity" the men rowed to the bank.

Two days later, on September 23, 1806, they reached St. Louis, then a mere frontier outpost. The whole town turned out to greet the heroes, cheering and toasting and wining and dining them.

Lewis hurried off a letter to President Jefferson: "In obedience to your orders we have penitrated the Continent of North America to the Pacific Ocean, and sufficiently explored the interior of the country to affirm with confidence that we have discovered the most practicable rout which dose exist across the continent." By water and land—not water alone—it was possible to reach the Pacific.

The expedition was over. The explorers had succeeded in their mission. They had carried out Jefferson's instructions, journeying some 8,000 miles to the Pacific and back, bringing with them a vast array of information on the flora, the fauna, the geology, and the inhabitants of the strange new world to the west—all at a cost to the Government of about $39,000.

Slowly the news spread. Jefferson, when he learned of the success of the expedition, expressed "unspeakable joy." He entertained Lewis and the Mandan contingent at a gala reception in the President's House. Clark did not attend. He was away in Virginia, wooing Julia Hancock, the girl for whom he had named a river and who soon would receive his name in marriage.

Lewis would never marry. Incredibly, tragically, only three years after he returned from the West in triumph, he died at the age of 35.

Historians are still debating the circumstances surrounding the explorer's death: Was it suicide or was it murder? Did Lewis take his own life in a fit of depression, or was he shot, robbed, and left to die on the Natchez Trace in 1809?

In that last year of his life, Lewis bore the obvious signs of a troubled man. As Governor of the Louisiana Territory, he had been constantly harassed by scheming men and continually disturbed by feuds and quarrels among the territory's officials.

Frederick Bates, the Virginia lawyer who was the territorial Secretary, had so disliked and resented the explorer that he privately tried to undermine his position. But worst of all, the sensitive Lewis felt that his honor had been impeached—Government auditors in Washington had refused to pay several of his vouchers.

Chief among these was one for $500, an amount Lewis had advanced to the St. Louis Missouri Fur Company to help get Big White back to his people. The cost of organizing an armed party of 125 men to escort the chief was $7,000, and the $500 extra was for gifts and bribes to Indians who might stop the party.

To Lewis it seemed a reasonable expense, considering that the Arikaras and Mandans were at war and that a previous attempt to get Big White back had failed.

Standing in a park before the grass-shrouded foundation of the crude log cabin where Lewis died, 60 miles from Nashville, Tennessee, I tried to piece together the events as they are known.

Lewis had decided to go to Washington to plead his case, to explain in person the necessity he felt for advancing the funds. The Government's failure to understand had weighed on him, and during the boat journey from the territorial headquarters in St. Louis to Fort Pickering, Tennessee, he also was in poor health.

In the words of Capt. Gilbert C. Russell, the commanding officer at Fort Pickering, Lewis had arrived at the post, near Memphis, in "a state of mental derangement." Members of the crew of Lewis's boat had informed Russell that the Governor had "made two attempts to kill himself" during the voyage.

Captain Russell detained Lewis until he appeared well enough to travel, and then on horseback Lewis continued toward Washington over the blazed Natchez Trace. With him rode James Neelly, an Indian agent Lewis had met at the fort, Neelly's servant, and a servant Lewis had brought with him from St. Louis.

About sunset on October 10, 1809, the weary Governor rode up to the traveler's rest cabin called Grinder's Stand. Neelly had hung behind to hunt for two stray pack horses; when he arrived the following day Meriwether Lewis was dead.

In a painful letter to Jefferson, Neelly tried to explain what had happened: When Lewis had reached the Stand, its owner, Robert Grinder, was away, but Mrs. Grinder was there. Discovering the Governor "to be deranged," she gave up the main cabin and went to one nearby to sleep while the servants slept in the stable.

"The woman reports that about three o'Clock she heard two pistols fire off in the Governors Room: the servants being awakined by her, came in but too late to save him," Neelly wrote the former President. "He had shot himself in the head with one pistol & a little below the Breast with

"...we came in Sight of the little french Village... the men raised a Shout and Sprung upon their ores.... they discharged 3 rounds with a harty cheer, which was returned from five tradeing boats...."

From the journal of Captain Clärk, September 20, 1806, as the expedition reached La Charrette, near St. Charles

the other—when his servant came in he says; I have done the business my good Servant give me some water."

The wounded Lewis had staggered out of the cabin, then returned, and stumbled out again.

Mrs. Grinder was quoted later as saying the dying man begged the servants "to take his rifle and blow out his brains, and he would give them all the money he had in his trunk. He often said, 'I am no coward; but I am so strong, so hard to die.'"

Jefferson never doubted that Lewis had committed suicide. He recalled that his former secretary long had suffered from "hypocondriac affections. ... While he lived with me in Washington, I observed at times sensible depressions of mind."

Yet passing years have brought arguments for murder. About $100 was missing from Lewis's effects and never found; perhaps Lewis, like many others before him, had fallen victim to bandits who roamed the Natchez Trace. Lewis's signs of derangement might simply have been malaria, some have reasoned, and the Grinders themselves might have been involved, others have theorized.

Clearly, no firm case can be made either for suicide or murder. The evidence is too circumstantial, too inconclusive.

I cannot help feeling that Lewis was the kind of man who might very well have taken his own life. He was happiest as an explorer. Since childhood he had loved to wander alone in the woods and fields. Meriwether Lewis was not a man cut out to be an administrator, to sit behind a desk. In such a position he could never have been content.

FROM THE SITE of the old cabin I walked with my family to Lewis's grave, about 700 feet away. A broken stone shaft created to symbolize a life shattered in its prime marks the spot, and here I read aloud from the inscription that paraphrases the words of his friend Thomas Jefferson: "His courage was undaunted; his firmness and perseverance yielded to nothing but impossibilities."

For years after Lewis's death, tears would come to Clark's eyes whenever he spoke of his partner in discovery. On first hearing the tragic news, he had moaned, "I fear O! I fear the weight of his mind has overcome him." But later he came to accept the murder theory.

Like his partner, Clark had received 1,600 acres of land as a reward for his role in leading the expedition, plus $1,228 in double pay. He resigned with relish the insulting lieutenant's commission he received at the start of the venture. His talents recognized, he was appointed a Brigadier General of Militia of Louisiana and also Superintendent of Indian Affairs for the territory.

Then in 1813 he was appointed Governor of the Missouri Territory, a position comparable to the one that Lewis held at the time of his death. Clark held this post until 1821, when Missouri became a state. Julia had died the year before after 12 years of marriage, having borne four sons and a daughter. Clark soon remarried, and of this union came two more sons. He died in St. Louis in 1838 at age 68.

Clark did not forget the promise he had made to Charbonneau and Sacagawea. He knew she "desirved a greater reward for her attention and services on that rout than we had in our power to give her at the Mandans." And in 1810, when Charbonneau and Sacagawea brought Jean Baptiste to him, he took charge of the youngster and put him in school.

In 1824 Baptiste met the visiting German Prince Paul of Württemberg and traveled with him in Europe. Eventually he became an interpreter and guide among the Indians; one of the white men he later guided was Clark's own son Jefferson. He died in Oregon in 1885 at the age of 80.

In her lifetime, Sacagawea received none of the glory that would later make her one of the most heroic women in American history. Though there is a popular belief that she lived to the age of 100 and died in the Wind River country of central Wyoming, more substantial evidence points to a much earlier demise.

Clark had kept in close touch with the family for years, and about 1828, while listing the members of the expedition, he had penned clearly, "Se car ja we au Dead."

Charbonneau did live to old age, eventually vanishing from the prairies of the upper Missouri, where he had served as a Government interpreter among the Mandans.

Except for the deserter Reed, each of the men of the permanent party received double his back pay and 320 acres of land from the Government. Many soon sold their claims, and though Clark tried to keep in touch with them, over the years they scattered across the country.

Clark gave York his freedom and reportedly set him up in the freight-hauling business with a wagon and a team of six horses; not long after, the former slave died, apparently of cholera, in Tennessee.

Drouillard joined a fur-trading expedition of the Spanish trader Manuel Lisa in 1807, and was tried and acquitted of killing a deserter. He died two years later of wounds suffered in an encounter with Blackfoot Indians near the Three Forks.

Two other members of the Lewis and Clark Expedition also were killed by Blackfeet—Pvt. John Potts in 1808 and Cruzatte in the mid-1820's. Others escaped with their lives in different scrapes.

Frazer got into debt and once attacked a sheriff who tried to arrest him. Shannon, after much suffering, lost a leg shattered in an unsuccessful attempt to return Big White to his Mandan home, a feat finally accomplished by others in 1809.

In 1810 Clark sent Shannon to Philadelphia to help lawyer Nicholas Biddle prepare a narrative of the expedition for eventual publication in 1814. Shannon later married and became a judge before his death in 1836 at the age of 51.

Of the sergeants, Ordway settled down with a wife in Missouri and became a prosperous landowner; for his journal, finally published in 1916, the captains had paid him $300. Pryor served in the War of 1812, became an Indian trader, married an Osage, and died among her people in 1831. Gass also served in the War of 1812, lost an eye, married at 60, and had seven children; he was nearly 99 when he died in 1870, the last recorded survivor of the expedition except for Sacagawea's son.

Gass's journal, printed in 1807, became the first published account of the expedition. Last of the narratives to reach print were the field notes Clark kept up to the land of the Mandans. Discovered in 1953 in an attic in St. Paul, Minnesota, these papers finally were published 11 years later after a lengthy legal argument over their ownership.

Little is known about most of the others of the proud band of 29 who completed the journey to St. Louis. By 1828 Clark had listed nine more of them dead — Collins, McNeal, Shields, Thompson, Wiser, Goodrich, Gibson, Jean Baptiste Lepage, and Joseph Field. Reuben lived longer, but just when he died no one knows.

Into similar obscurity vanished many more — Hall, Howard, Labiche, Whitehouse, Windsor, and Werner among them.

After wandering the West with his two fellow fur trappers, Colter joined the St. Louis Missouri Fur Company, and in 1807-08, while traveling alone in search of Indians with whom to trade, he became the first known white American to penetrate the country that today forms Yellowstone National Park.

Yet he is remembered as well for a foot race. In 1808, near the Three Forks of the Missouri, he and Potts were attacked by Blackfeet. Potts was killed and Colter seized, stripped naked, and sent running for his life before a band of howling Indians. Miraculously, he escaped and eventually reached the safety of a fort.

He later settled down at La Charrette and married. In 1813 he died of jaundice, his exploits unsung.

So ALL OF THEM were gone — this whole band of superlative explorers. Traveling in their footsteps, I had seen them at their best, sharing with them their hopes, fears, joys, and disappointments. And in searching to rediscover the land that they had known, I developed a new and deeper understanding of the Nation they had helped to build.

In the wake of their exploits would come many changes. Soon the covered wagon would wend its way westward, then the stagecoach and the railroad. And highways one day would supersede rivers as principal arteries of transportation. The great plains would be tilled and planted, and the hum and thunder of giant industries would echo through towns and cities and across meadows and plains.

But whatever was to happen, whatever was to follow, the deeds of the men of the Corps of Discovery would stand forever. The names of the leaders of the expedition would become inseparably linked in history: The story of their exploits would become an American legend.

Others would follow. But Lewis and Clark had been the first. And never again would the West be the same.

Partners in discovery, Lewis and Clark now rest far apart. At St. Louis, Clark's tomb reflects a life crowned with success. Lewis met a mystery-shrouded end at Grinder's Stand in the Tennessee hills. His gravestone there bears words adapted from Jefferson's eulogy.

GERALD S. SNYDER, NATIONAL GEOGRAPHIC STAFF (LOWER)

CHANGING RIVERS ERASE HISTORIC SITES

Washington's Lower Monumental Dam—one among many on the Snake River—impounds water to supply power and to permit navigation into Idaho. Along the course of Lewis and Clark's journey only infrequent stretches of waterway remain in their original, unharnessed state. Today a ribbonlike expanse of reservoirs serves the needs of growing cities, drowning countless old landmarks.

CONQUERING THE WESTERN PLAINS

Blackfoot warriors in bronze swoop to the attack in Robert Scriver's vigorous sculpture, recalling the once warlike zest of Indian life on the now peaceful plains. Near Great Falls, Montana, a wheat harvester (top left) gathers in the crop. Patterned folds of plowed earth replace wild sagebrush in eastern Washington. A factory along the Mississippi (below left) sends up signals of industry at work.

REMINDERS OF THE MANDANS

At Fort Lincoln State Park the North Dakota wind sweeps a reconstructed Mandan village, a memorial to a vanished people. Here, in a mounded earth lodge, the author and his family kept Christmas. Cottonwood logs blazed, and buffalo ribs sizzled on the fire, kindling thoughts of Lewis and Clark's winter among the Mandans. In a scene painted by Bodmer (left) a Mandan worshiper stands before his lords of life—crude figures of the sun and moon raised on poles—praying for good fortune in hunt and harvest. In the end such entreaties proved useless: Epidemics of smallpox spread through villages, virtually snuffing out the tribe.

IDAHO'S UNTAMED SALMON RIVER
REMAINS A CHALLENGE

Wild and wintry, the Salmon River tumbles through its deep granite gorge, leaping over falls, frothing down rapids. Past snow patches skillful boatmen ride white water coursing through Idaho's national forests. Rugged terrain like the rocky Salmon Falls whirlpool (left) forced the expedition to seek an alternate route through the mountains. Conservationists hope to win protection for the stream under the 1968 Wild and Scenic Rivers Act, thus preserving a primitive fastness.

YESTERDAY'S FRONTIER

Fourth of July fireworks burst over the skyline of St. Louis, frontier hub of the early Republic. In September 1806 the town's residents turned out en masse to celebrate the safe return of the Corps of Discovery. Curving gracefully 630 feet above the city's Mississippi riverfront, Gateway Arch honors those men and women who followed in the footsteps of Lewis and Clark.

Index

Illustrations references, including legends, appear in *italics*

Roster of the Lewis and Clark Expedition

CO-LEADERS: Meriwether Lewis, Captain, 1st U. S. Infantry, and William Clark, commissioned 2nd Lieutenant, U. S. Corps of Artillerists,
but considered equal to Lewis in rank and command during the expedition to the Pacific and back.

SERGEANTS: Charles Floyd (died August 20, 1804), Patrick Gass (a
private when Floyd died; elected to succeed Floyd August 22, 1804),
John Ordway, and Nathaniel Pryor.

PRIVATES OF THE PERMANENT PARTY: William Bratton, John Collins,
John Colter, Pierre Cruzatte, Joseph Field, Reuben Field, Robert
Frazer, George Gibson, Silas Goodrich, Hugh Hall, Thomas Procter
Howard, Francis Labiche, Jean Baptiste Lepage (a trader recruited at
Fort Mandan), Hugh McNeal, John Potts, George Shannon, John
Shields, John B. Thompson, William Werner, Joseph Whitehouse,
Alexander Willard, Richard Windsor, and Peter Wiser.

SOLDIERS WHO JOURNEYED ONLY AS FAR AS FORT MANDAN: Cpl.
Richard Warfington and Pvts. John Boley, John Dame, John Newman,
Moses B. Reed, Ebenezer Tuttle, and Isaac White. Originally members of the permanent party, Newman and Reed were court-martialed
and sent back to St. Louis.

CIVILIANS OF THE EXPEDITION: George Drouillard, Toussaint Charbonneau (hired as an interpreter at Fort Mandan), his wife Sacagawea,
their son Jean Baptiste (born February 11, 1805), and Clark's slave
York. The record is not clear concerning the names and number of
the French engagés hired by Lewis and Clark; possibly ten traveled
with the expedition as far as Fort Mandan.

Acknowledgments

The Special Publications Division is grateful to the people named or quoted in the text and to those listed here for their generous cooperation and assistance during the preparation of this book: Howard I. Chapelle (boats), John C. Ewers (Indians), Craddock R. Goins, Jr. (military history), M. H. Jackson (boats), Donald E. Kloster (military history), Deanna Love (costumes), Velva E. Rudd (botany), and Henry W. Setzer (mammals), all Smithsonian Institution; George R. Brooks and staff of the Missouri Historical Society; Richard S. Brownlee, State Historical Society of Missouri; Gus Budde, National Park Service, St. Louis, Mo.; Dayton W. Canaday, South Dakota Historical Society; Clarence H. Decker, Illinois Lewis and Clark Committee; Mildred D. Downing, Clearwater Historical Museum; Detmar H. Finke, Office of the Chief of Military History, Washington, D. C.; Sherry R. Fisher, 1964-69 Lewis and Clark Trail Commission; Sam Gilluly and staff of the Montana Historical Society; Mildred Goosman, Joslyn Art Museum; Archibald Hanna, Jr., Yale University; Gertrude D. Hess, American Philosophical Society; Clyde Jones, Fish and Wildlife Service; Robert Killen, Nebraska Game and Parks Commission; Kenneth M. Long, U. S. Army Corps of Engineers; John McMillan, Oregon Historical Society; Uuno M. Sahinen, Montana Bureau of Mines and Geology; Frank A. Sandvig, Beaverhead National Forest; Ralph S. Space, Orofino, Idaho; Gail Stensland, Upper Missouri Wilderness Waterway Cruise Company, Fort Benton, Montana; Ralph S. Thompson, North Dakota Lewis and Clark Advisory Committee; Willis Van Devanter, The Brick House, Upperville, Va.; Charles van Ravenswaay, Winterthur Museum; Joseph Watterson, National Park Service; E. Winston Woolfolk, Caroline County Historical Association.

   The staff wishes to thank Mr. and Mrs. Paul Mellon for granting permission to photograph plates from *Illustrations to Maximilian, Prince of Wied's Travels in the Interior of North America,* 1844, and George Catlin, *O-kee-pa; a Religious Ceremony; and other Customs of the Mandans,* 1867.

Bibliography

The reader may wish to refer to the following books for further reading: JOURNALS, LETTERS, AND DOCUMENTS: Gass, Patrick, *A Journal of the Voyages and Travels of a Corps of Discovery,* 1958; Jackson, Donald, *Letters of the Lewis and Clark Expedition With Related Documents, 1783-1854,* 1962; Nasatir, Abraham P., *Before Lewis and Clark: Documents Illustrating the History of the Missouri, 1785-1804* (2 volumes), 1952; Osgood, Ernest Staples, *The Field Notes of Captain William Clark, 1803-1805,* 1964; Quaife, Milo M., *The Journals of Captain Meriwether Lewis and Sergeant John Ordway,* 1916; Thwaites, Reuben Gold, *Original Journals of the Lewis and Clark Expedition* (8 volumes), 1959. GENERAL: Andrist, Ralph K., *To the Pacific With Lewis and Clark,* 1967; Bakeless, John, *Lewis and Clark: Partners in Discovery,* 1947; DeVoto, Bernard, *The Course of Empire,* 1952; Dillon, Richard H., *Meriwether Lewis,* 1965; Eide, Ingvard Henry, *American Odyssey: The Journey of Lewis and Clark,* 1969; Malone, Dumas, *Jefferson the President,* 1970; Wheeler, Olin D., *The Trail of Lewis and Clark, 1804-1904* (2 volumes), 1904. INDIANS: Catlin, George, *Illustrations of the Manners, Customs, and Condition of the North American Indians* (2 volumes), 1866; Donaldson, Thomas, *The George Catlin Indian Gallery in the U. S. National Museum,* 1887; Ewers, John C., *Artists of the Old West,* 1965; Smithsonian Institution, *Handbook of American Indians North of Mexico* (2 volumes), 1907; Kane, Paul, *Wanderings of an Artist Among the Indians of North America,* 1968; Lowie, Robert H., *Indians of the Plains,* 1954; Renner, Frederic G., *Charles M. Russell: Paintings, Drawings, and Sculpture in the Amon G. Carter Collection,* 1966; Ross, Marvin C., *The West of Alfred Jacob Miller,* 1968; Wilson, Gilbert L., *The Hidatsa Earthlodge,* 1934. NATURAL HISTORY: Branch, E. Douglas, *The Hunting of the Buffalo,* 1962; Burroughs, Raymond Darwin, *The Natural History of the Lewis and Clark Expedition,* 1961; Cutright, Paul R., *Lewis and Clark, Pioneering Naturalists,* 1969; Haines, Francis, *The Buffalo,* 1970.

Composition for *In the Footsteps of Lewis and Clark* by National Geographic's Phototypographic Division, John E. McConnell, Manager. Printed and bound by Fawcett Printing Corporation, Rockville, Md. Color separations by Beck Engraving Co., Philadelphia, Pa.; Graphic Color Plate, Inc., Stamford, Conn.; The Lanman Co., Alexandria, Va.; Lebanon Valley Offset, Inc., Cleona, Pa.; and Progressive Color Corporation, Rockville, Md.

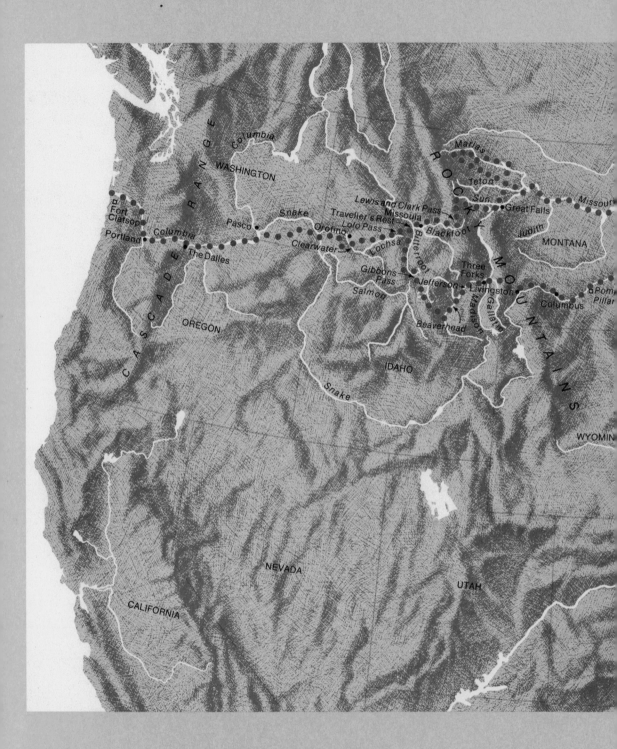

THE HOMEWARD ROUTE OF THE

On March 23, 1806—after four dreary months at Fort Clatsop—the explorers started home, retracing their route up the Columbia. On horseback, they bypassed the Snake and once again headed into the Bitterroots. The expedition split up at Traveller's Rest—Lewis taking one